A quick beginners' course in spoken Mandarin for holidaymakers and business people

Course writer and producer
Katherine Flower, BBC Radio, Continuing Education

Consultant
Liu Xia, Senior Producer, BBC External Services Chinese Section

Adviser
Ma Yuan He, Central China Television

BBC Books

Get by in Chinese
A BBC Radio course
First broadcast in Autumn 1988

Published to accompany a series
of programmes prepared in
consultation with the BBC
Educational Broadcasting Council

Acknowledgements

Special thanks to Donna Wilson
for all her help in preparing the
radio programmes, book and
cassettes, and to Alan Wilding for
many good ideas and much
encouragement

Illustrations by Alan Burton
Cover designed by Peter Bridgewater and Annie Moss

Published by BBC Books, a division of BBC Enterprises Ltd,
Woodlands, 80 Wood Lane, London W12 0TT

ISBN 0 563 39951 1
First published in 1988
This edition published in 1995

Printed and bound in Great Britain by Clays Ltd, St Ives plc
Cover printed by Clays Ltd, St Ives plc

Contents

CHINA
HEILONGJIANG
Harbin
JILIN
Jilin City
Shenyang
LIAONING
INNER MONGOLIA
Urumqi
Dunhuang
XINJIANG
Kashgar
GANSU
NINGXIA
Hohhot
PEKING
HEBEI
Xiyang
SHANXI
Jinan
SHANDONG
QINGHAI
Xian
Yellow River
JIANSU
SHAANXI
HENAN
Nanking
Shanghai
XIZANG (TIBET)
HUBEI
ANHUI
Shaoxing
Chengdu
Yangtze
River
Wuhan
ZHEJAING
Himalayas
Lhasa
Chongqing
SICHUAN
Nanchang
Mt Everest
HUNAN
JIANGXI
FUJIAN
GUIZHOU
Mekong River
TAIWAN
Autonomous regions
Great Wall
Kunming
Guilin
GUANGDONG
Canton
YUNNAN
GUANGXI
Hong Kong

Welcome to China

China is the third largest country in the world after the USSR and the USA, with terrain ranging from Everest, the world's highest mountain (known as Qoomalama to the Chinese), to the Takla Makan desert, one of the most barren areas to be found anywhere. It includes steppe, forest, temperate seashore and sub-tropical jungle. It also has over a billion people to feed and clothe, almost one quarter of the world's population. About 93 per cent of the people are Han, or ethnic Chinese; the remaining 68 million are made up of 55 'minority nationalities', mostly scattered in the sparsely populated border areas. Five of these areas – Inner Mongolia, Ningxia, Xinjiang, Xizang (Tibet) and Guangxi – are autonomous regions.

The Chinese sense of their own history is very strong. Probably the best-known dynasties in the West are the Qin dynasty (221-207 BC), which was responsible for building the Great Wall and the famous tomb in Xian where 7000 terracotta warriors stand in silent vigil over the dead emperor; the Tang dynasty (AD 618-907), generally considered to be one of the best periods in Chinese history for art and poetry; and the last imperial dynasty, the Qing dynasty (1644-1911). In 1911, Sun Yat Sen, influenced by Christianity and Western concepts of liberalism, overthrew the Qing dynasty and formed the first Republic; and until the Communist takeover of power in 1949, there was a great deal of political and military confusion in the country. Japanese pressure increased steadily from 1931 when Manchuria became a Japanese protectorate, and the Japanese installed a puppet emperor, Pu Yi, the last emperor of China, who had been deposed (but not harmed) in 1911. For a brief while, the Communists and the Guomindang, under Chiang Kai Shek, united to form an anti-Japanese resistance; and when, after the bombing of Pearl Harbor in 1941, the Japanese invasion of China became part of the larger world conflict, the Chinese also had the help of the Allied Forces. In 1945, the battle against the Japanese was at last won; but the civil war in China continued until 1949 when the remnants of Chiang Kai Shek's army fled to Taiwan.

1 October 1949 saw the proclamation of the People's Republic of China – and Chinese history since then has been marked by various campaigns and initiatives as different 'roads to Communism' have been tried, with varying degrees of success. In 1966, the 'Great Proletarian Cultural Revolution' was launched by an ageing, and increasingly unwell, Mao Ze Dong; it came to an end ten years later with Mao's death and the arrest a few days later of his widow, Jiang Qing, and the other members of what became known as the 'Gang of Four'. The Cultural Revolution left millions dead and millions more displaced, numbed from the shock of what they had been through. China started to open up to the West again, and to repair the damaged buildings and damaged lives that the 'ten years of chaos', as the Chinese now refer to it, had left in their wake.

Nowadays, with the exception only of a few sensitive border regions, most areas are open to foreign back-packers and business people alike: gone are the days when travelling more than 30 kilometres outside a town necessitated a special permit from the public security police, with a detailed timetable of your movements. Under Deng Xiao Ping, the Open Door policy has become not just another slogan but a reality, with an unparalleled opening-up of the country which continues at all levels. In 1986, 1.5 million tourists visited China, and to that figure can be added countless 'overseas Chinese' going to visit relatives, as well as business people, students, politicians, pop stars, football teams, scientists and film-makers. To take advantage fully of the opportunities to travel in China, it is essential to know some *pǔtōnghùa*, standard (Mandarin) Chinese: many Chinese are studying English but some knowledge of their language is not only polite but vital, especially outside big cities, and will be much appreciated.

Why Mandarin?

The one place your new knowledge of Mandarin may not be useful is in your local Chinese restaurant, where the proprietors will most likely speak Cantonese, the language of South China, or possibly Fukkienese, Hakka or a similar southern Chinese dialect. In most countries with a large Chinese population – Malaysia, Indonesia, Singapore, the Philippines – the spoken languages are from South China. However, most speakers of Chinese do understand Mandarin. In Taiwan, Mandarin is the main language, and many Hong Kong Chinese (mostly speakers of Cantonese) are learning it in preparation for their territory's return to China in 1997. *Pǔtōnghùa* is based upon the dialect of Beijing, the capital of China. It gradually became accepted as the official national language during the first Republic (1912-1949), but has had most impact since radio, the cinema and, later, TV became widespread. There are still wide variations in local accent and dialect (for example, Shanghai's 13 million people speak *Shànghǎihùa* which is more or less incomprehensible to non-Shanghainese). But if you speak *pǔtōnghùa*, you will 'get by' everywhere in China.

The Script

Since 1949, the People's Republic of China has simplified many complex characters but Chinese script is still immensely complex and even Chinese people are likely to come across a character they do not know when they are reading a book. Although it is generally reckoned that literacy consists of a knowledge of between three and four thousand characters, there are many more characters than this, especially in the realms of poetry, science and so on, and each character can combine with many others to make compound words. Nevertheless, the Chinese script unites China: speakers of *pǔtōnghùa* will not always understand other dialects of Chinese but an understanding of the script is universal, regardless of the variation in the spoken language.

Learning the characters is, of course, a slow and painstaking process and children copy each one hundreds of times; nowadays children at primary school first learn to read and write *pīnyīn*, the romanised system of writing down Chinese characters. This is also an aid to using dictionaries, phone directories and, these days, computers. It is doubtful whether *pīnyīn* can ever replace the characters; but for the non-Chinese student of the language who does not have the time or courage to tackle the characters, it means there is a standardised way of writing down Chinese words which is quick and easy to learn. *Pīnyīn* is even used on shop signs and advertising posters. While this is probably invisible to the Chinese, who only 'see' the characters, it is a great encouragement to the baffled foreigner.

In this book, only *pīnyīn* is used. It is possible to speak good Chinese without knowing a single character but there may be times when it is useful to know how a character is written (for example, when you are reading a menu or writing the destination of a letter). For this a pocket dictionary, with the words written in characters as well as in *pīnyīn*, will be invaluable so that you can say the word and, *in extremis*, point to the characters, just in case someone doesn't understand.

Pronunciation

Pīnyīn is a phonetic system of transliterating the sound each Chinese character makes. Most letters are read more or less as in English, but there are a few peculiarities. The examples are on the cassette for you to practise:

Example:	c [like *ts* in ca*ts*]	càidān – menu
	h [like Lo*ch* Ness]	hěn – very
	q [like *ch* in *ch*eap]	qǐng – please
	r [similar to the English 'r' but the tip of the tongue is turned up and touches the roof of the mouth]	rén – person
	x [like *sh* in *sh*eep]	xiǎo – small, young
	z [like *ds* in li*ds*]	zài jiàn – goodbye
	zh [like *j* in *j*ug]	zhèr – here
	j [like *zh* but softer]	jǐ diǎn? – what time?

Tones

Mandarin has four tones. To the western ear it can be almost impossible to hear the difference between them without hours and hours of painstaking practice. To a Chinese the change from, say, the word *mài* (falling tone) meaning 'sell', and *mǎi* (falling-rising tone) meaning 'buy', is as clear as the difference between 'buy' and 'sell' to us. All the Chinese words printed in this book are marked with accents indicating the tonal value of each word:

- ¯ first tone: high, neither rising or falling
- ´ second tone: rising
- ˘ third tone: falling-rising
- ` fourth tone: falling

NOTE: Every syllable is pronounced in one of these four tones unless it is unstressed – in this case the tone distinction disappears, and in the text unstressed syllables do not have a tone mark over them. Listen carefully to both individual words and to the intonation of words within phrases, and try to copy them as closely as possible. The following tone drills are on the cassette and will help your awareness of the differences between tones:

1st tone (high)	2nd tone (rising)	3rd tone (falling-rising)	4th tone (falling)
mā (mother)	*má* (pins and needles)	*mă* (horse)	*mà* (swear)
xī (west)	*xí* (straw mat)	*xĭ* (happiness)	*xì* (play)
nān (child – South China only)	*nán* (south)	*năn* (to be embarrassed)	*nàn* (hardship)
chāng (prosperous)	*cháng* (long)	*chăng* (place)	*chàng* (to sing)
chī (eat)	*chí* (to be late)	*chĭ* (ruler, measuring stick)	*chì* (naked)
chā (fork)	*chá* (tea)	*chă* (shorts)	*chà* (to lag behind)

N.B. The English meanings given above are not the only possible ones – most of these words have several other meanings as well.

1 Greetings

Key expressions

Nǐ hǎo!	Hullo
Nǐmen hǎo!	Hullo (to two or more people)
Wǒ xìng Liu	My (family) name is Liu
Wǒ shì Yīngguórén	I'm English
Wǒ bù shì Yīngguórén	I'm not English
Tā shì Zhōngguórén ma?	Is he/she Chinese?

Conversations

Liu and Wang meet in the street

LIU: Nǐ hǎo![1]
WANG: Nǐ hǎo!

Liu meets Wang and Xu in the park

LIU: Nǐmen hǎo![1]
WANG AND XU: Nǐ hǎo, Liu.

Liu meets Li and Deng. They know each other already

LIU: Nǐmen hǎo!
LI: Nǐ hǎo, Xiǎo Liu.[2]
DENG: Xiǎo Liu – nǐ hǎo!

Liu Dai Lin introduces herself to Wang Bao Qing

LIU: Nǐ hǎo! Wǒ xìng Liu . . . Liu Dai Lin.[3]
WANG: Nǐ hǎo, Liu! Wǒ xìng Wang . . . Wang Bao Qing.

Anne Wilson introduces herself to Lao Wang

ANNE: Nǐ hǎo! Wǒ xìng Wilson . . . Anne Wilson.
WANG: Nǐ hǎo Wilson . . . Wǒ xìng Wang . . . Lǎo Wang.[2]

Zhang Hua meets Anne and wants to know if she's American

ZHANG: Nǐ hǎo! Nǐ shì Měiguórén ma?[4]
ANNE: Bù.[5] Wǒ shì Yīngguórén.[6] Nǐ ne?
ZHANG: Wǒ shì Zhōngguórén. Wǒ xìng Zhang.
ANNE: Nǐ hǎo Zhang. Wǒ xìng Wilson.

Anne, Wang and Liu meet and find out where each one comes from

WANG: Nǐ hǎo – wǒ xìng Wang – Lǎo Wang-ah.
ANNE: Nǐ hǎo, Lǎo Wang!
WANG: Nǐ shì Měiguórén ma?
ANNE: Bù. Wǒ shì Yīngguórén. Nǐ shì Shànghǎirén ma?
WANG: Shì-ah. Zhè shì Liu Dai Lin – Xiǎo Liu.
ANNE: Nǐ hǎo, Xiǎo Liu! Nǐ yě shì Shànghǎirén ma?
LIU: Bù shì. Wǒ shì Běijīngrén. Huānyíng nǐ dào Shànghǎi lái!
ANNE: Xiè xie, xiè xie nǐ.

Jenny meets Feng Cun Li and his son, Shen Shen

JENNY: Xiǎo Feng! Nǐ hǎo!
FENG CUN LI: Jenny, nǐ hǎo!
JENNY: Nǐ hǎo, xiǎo péngyǒu!
SHEN SHEN: Āyí hǎo![7] Nǐ shì wàiguórén ma?
JENNY: Wǒ bù shì wàiguórén – wǒ shì Yīngguó huáqiáo.[8]
SHEN SHEN: Yīngguó huáqiáo . . .?
JENNY: Xiǎo péngyǒu, nǐ xìng shénme-ah?
SHEN SHEN: Wǒ? Wǒ xìng Feng . . . Feng Shen Shen. Āyí huānyíng nǐ dào Běijīng, lái.
JENNY: Xiè xie nǐ, Shen Shen.

Explanations

1 Greetings

Nǐ hǎo means 'hullo' (literally, you – fine). *Nǐmen hǎo* also means 'hullo' and is used when you are speaking to two or more people. (*Nǐmen* is the plural form of 'you'.)

2 Forms of address

Xiǎo Liu – 'young Liu'. After meeting someone for the first time, you can put *Xiǎo* in front of their surname if they are under about 35 or if they are much younger than you.

Lǎo Wang – 'old Wang'. Similarly, you can politely address someone, say, 10 years or more older than yourself, or anyone over about 40, by using *Lǎo* plus their surname.

3 Names and forms of address

Mao Ze Dong – Mao is the family name and Ze Dong his given name. By the way, if you meet anyone who is as venerable as, say, Deng Xiao Ping, you can call them *Deng Lǎo* – the word *Lǎo* goes after the surname as a mark of very great respect.

Some Chinese people have only one given name, not two, e.g. Zhang Hua. (*Zhang* is the surname and *Hua* is the given name.) It is usual with a name like this to call the person by their full name – not *Xiǎo Zhang* or *Lǎo Zhang*, but simply *Zhang Hua*.

Unless you know a Chinese person very well, don't use their given name on its own.

Children up to about 15 often have 'doubled' pet names like Lili, Yiyi, Shen Shen. After about 15, they graduate to *Xiǎo* plus their surname.

Chinese people use *tóngzhì* ('comrade') in very specialised situations, like addressing a soldier of the P.L.A. (People's Liberation Army). As a general rule, don't use it until you know China very well. In China, you will hear the phrase *tóngzhìmen hǎo!* ('hullo comrades!') on the radio, TV and loudspeaker announcements at railway stations – the plural is formed by adding *-men* to the end of the word, just as the plural of *nǐ* ('you') is formed by adding *-men* (*nǐmen*).

The words *xiānsheng* ('mister'), *xiáojie* ('miss') and *tàitai* ('madame') were considered bourgeois for a long time but are now coming back into use. They are used by Chinese towards foreigners to be polite. If you want to be extra polite when you meet someone for the first time, you could say:
Nǐ hǎo, Liu xiáojie (Miss Liu)
Wang xiānsheng (Mr Wang)
Zhang tàitai (Madame Zhang)
After you have met someone a couple of times, you progress to Lǎo and Xiǎo. In addition, *xiáojie* can be used to attract the attention of a waitress or a female shop assistant, while *xiānsheng* can be used to call a waiter or a male shop assistant.

4 Questions

Some things <u>are</u> difficult in Chinese; but forming questions is not one of them! Simply add *ma* to a sentence, plus a question mark or question intonation, and you have a question. The other way of forming questions (equally simple) is dealt with in unit 6.

5 Negatives

To make a sentence negative, simple put *bù* in front of the verb:
Wǒ shì Zhōngguórén I'm Chinese
Wǒ bù shì Zhōngguórén I'm not Chinese

There is no exact word for 'no' in Chinese. If you

want to say 'no' in answer to a question, you can either add *bù* to the verb used in the question, or you can say *bù* alone:
Nǐ dào Shànghǎi qù ma? Are you going to Shanghai?
Bù. No.
Bù qù. No, I'm not going.

6 Nationality

To say your nationality, add the word *rén* ('person') to the name of your country:
Yīngguó England
Wǒ shì Yīngguórén I'm English

You can do the same with Chinese cities:
Wǒ shì Shànghǎirén I'm from Shanghai

7 Children

Chinese children say *āyí* ('auntie') and *shūshu* ('uncle') to adults:
Āyí hǎo! – 'Hullo auntie!' *Shūshu hǎo!* – 'Hullo uncle!'

Similarly, adults often call children 'little friend' (*xiǎo péngyǒu*).

8 Overseas Chinese

Anyone who has Chinese origins is considered to be a *huáqiáo*, or overseas Chinese. For example, Jenny Lo, born in Britain of Singaporean parents, would not be a *Yīngguórén*, but a *Yīngguó huáqiáo* (an England – overseas Chinese).

Additional words and phrases

xiǎo young, little
lǎo old
tóngzhì comrade
xīansheng mister
xiáojie miss
tàitai madame, mrs
Yīngguó England
Měiguó USA
Fǎguó France
Déguó Germany
Zhōngguó China
Sūgelán Scotland
Àiěrlán Ireland
Wēiěrshi Wales
wàiguó foreign
huáqiáo overseas Chinese

rén person
yě also
huānyíng welcome
xiè xie (nǐ) thanks (thank you)
shénme? what?
péngyǒu friend
zài jiàn goodbye
dǎo to
ne? how about?
lái to come, to arrive

Verbs *Shì* ('to be') Like all Chinese verbs, *shì* does not change in form:

Wǒ		I am	Wǒmen		We are
Nǐ	shì	You are	Nǐmen	shì	You (pl) are
Tā		He/she/it is	Tāmen		They are

Exercises

1 Say hullo to:

(a) Wang and Liu, for the first time.
(b) Liu, age 29, on your second meeting.
(c) Zhang, age 60, whom you met yesterday.
(d) Deng Xiao Ping.

2 Say what each person is called, and what their nationality is:

a) Name: *Anna Thomas* Nationality: *English*

b) Name: *Marcel Dupont* Nationality: *French*

c) Name: *Sam Wang* Nationality: *American* (Parents: Chinese)

d) Name: *Li Cun Li* Nationality: *Chinese*

3 Ask:

(a) Are you American?
(b) Are you an overseas Chinese?
(c) Are you from Shanghai?

4 What do you say in answer to these questions:

(a) Nǐ shì Měiguórén ma?

(b) Tā (your partner) shì Yīngguórén ma?

(c) Nǐ xìng shénme?

5 Fill in the blanks:

(a) Feng and Wang: Nǐ ______ Xiǎo Liu.
Liu: ______ hǎo, Lǎo Wang, Xiǎo Feng.

(b) Wang: Nǐ ______. Wǒ ______ Wang.
John: Nǐ ______. Wǒ ______ Wilson.

(c) Wang: Nǐ ______ Měiguó ______ ma?
John: ______. Wǒ ______ Yīngguó ______.

6 Make questions out of these statements:

(a) Tā shì Yīngguórén.

(b) Lǎo Wang shì Běijīngrén.

(c) Tāmen shì Zhōngguórén.

(d) Nǐ xìng Liu.

(e) Tāmen bù shì Měiguórén.

7 Use the model to make questions and give negative answers:

MODEL:	Richard – English?	No – French
YOU SAY:	Richard shì Yīngguórén ma?	Tā bù shì Yīngguórén – tā shì Făguórén.

(a) Anne – American? No – English

(b) Lao Wang – from Shanghai? No – from Tianjin

(c) They – from Beijing? No – from Nanjing

(d) You – French? No – German

Worth knowing

Getting to China

Nowadays Beijing, Shanghai and Guangzhou (Canton) are linked to almost every major international city by direct flights and almost every airline has an office in Beijing. There are still few, if any, bucket shop deals to China, but there are cheap fares to Hong Kong, and once in Hong Kong the ways of getting to China are numerous. There are daily flights from Hong Kong to many Chinese cities, and the more adventurous traveller can take the train into Guangzhou, or a boat to Shanghai, or simply take the train from Hung Hom Station in Kowloon to the Chinese border and walk across the footbridge. Hydrofoils are frequent, and the trip from Hong Kong to Guangzhou by hydrofoil through the South China Sea is a beautiful one. The *Trans-Siberian Express* is another way to enter or leave Beijing – starting from Beijing rather than Europe is considerably cheaper. But allow seven days for the journey to Moscow, and take plenty of food, and some good books.

What to take

You do not need collapsible canoes, pith helmets or tins of beans. China is well and truly geared to tourism these days and you can buy films, alcohol (very cheaply), chocolate, instant coffee, English language newspapers, all toiletries, pens, writing paper . . . Some of the 'luxury' items will not be available in villages and smaller towns – so stock up in the big cities if you're off to Mongolia or Tibet.

If you are working in China, take business cards with your name printed on one side in English, on the other in Chinese.

Vitamin pills are a good idea. It can occasionally be difficult to get fresh fruit and vegetables, and Westerners may find travel and daily life in China particularly tiring.

Anti-malarial tablets may be necessary, depending on the region and the time of year. Consult your doctor. Mosquito repellant and suntan oil are hard to find in China, so stock up on these before you leave home. Also take some good books – nightlife is almost non-existent.

2 Food and drink

Key expressions

Yǒu/Yǒude	There is/are
Yǒu yú ma?	Is there any fish?
Méiyǒu (le)	There isn't/aren't any (left)
Qǐng zuò	Please sit down
Qǐng gěi wǒ . . .	Please give me . . .
Qǐng děng yī xiàr	Please wait a moment
Yào jǐ píng?	How many bottles do you want?
Duì bù qǐ	Excuse me, sorry
Jǐ ge?	How many? (things, people/small numbers)
Sān wǎn mǐfàn	Three bowls of rice
Kěyǐ	It's possible/OK/fine

Conversations

In the restaurant: Wang and his friend Feng want to have lunch, but the restaurant is busy and they have to wait for a table.

WANG:	Xiáojie, nǐ hǎo.
WAITRESS:	Qǐng nǐmen děng yī xiàr.
WANG:	Hǎo . . . [10 minutes later]
WAITRESS:	Qǐng zuò zhèr.
WANG:	Xiè xie nǐ . . . yǒu[1] píjiǔ ma?
WAITRESS:	Yǒude[2] . . . wǒmen yǒu Shànghǎi píjiǔ.
WANG:	Hǎo . . . yǒu yú[3] ma?
WAITRESS:	Yú . . . yǒu.

WANG: Yǒu jiǎozi ma?
WAITRESS: Yǒude.
WANG: Hǎo – qǐng gěi wǒmen jiǎozi, mǐfàn, yú, qīngcài[4], hé píjiǔ. Xiè xie nǐ.

In the restaurant

WANG: Nǐ hǎo Jenny – Xiǎo Liu, nǐ hǎo. Xiáojie! Xiáojie!
WAITRESS: Qǐng děng yī xiàr.
WANG: Hǎo . . . [10 minutes later]
WAITRESS: Hǎo – qǐng zuò zhèr.
WANG: Xiè xie . . . yǒu píjiǔ ma?
WAITRESS: Yǒude – Shànghǎi píjiǔ. Shànghǎi píjiǔ hěn hǎo. Yào ma?[5]
WANG: Kěyǐ. Qǐng gěi wǒmen sān[6] píng[7].
WAITRESS: Hǎode – Hái yào ma?[8]
WANG: Jiǎozi yǒu ma?
WAITRESS: Yǒude.
WANG: Qǐng gěi wǒmen jiǎozi, yú, hé qīngcài.
WAITRESS: Mǐfàn, yào ma?
WANG: Mǐfàn bù yào.

Explanations

1 *Yǒu*

Yǒu covers both possession (*Wǒ yǒu yī bēi chá* 'I have a cup of tea') and the availability or otherwise of something (*Yǒu píjiǔ ma?* 'Is there any beer?').

Yǒu is the only Chinese verb which is negated by *méi* in the present tense – so *méiyǒu* means 'there is not'. (As we saw in unit 1, all other verbs use *bù* to express the negative.) *Méiyǒu* is used to say that something is unavailable and, like other verbs in Chinese, there's no need to repeat the noun:

Yǒu mǐfàn ma? Is there any rice?
Méiyǒu. There isn't.

The addition of *le* makes the expression a little stronger – roughly speaking, *méiyǒu* means 'there's none', while *méiyǒu le* means 'there's none left at all'. (More on the use of *le* in unit 5.)

(It's worth remembering that the demand on goods and services in China is huge: shops and restaurants do run out of things more often than in the West. If someone says *méiyǒu*, do not lose your temper: smile politely and enquire about alternatives.)

2 *-de*

The addition of *-de* can make a reply stronger:
Yǒu píjiǔ ma? Is there any beer?
Yǒude. Yes, there certainly is.

Tā shì Měiguórén ma? Is he American?
Shì. Yes, he is.
Shìde. Yes, he certainly is.

De is tagged on to *hǎo* ('good') for agreeing a little more strongly:
Hǎode, hǎode. Yes, fine, I quite agree.

3 *Yú*

There are dozens of different sorts of fish and hundreds of ways of preparing them – consult your dictionary for examples. But most restaurants will have only a few on their menu at any one time, and if you ask for 'fish' you will be served the Fish of the Day.

4 *Qīngcài*

You will need a good pocket dictionary to cover all the sorts of vegetables which you will find in China. You will find, though, that the word *cài* occurs at the end of the name for many sorts of vegetables – for instance, *bái cài* (literally, 'white vegetable') is what we call Chinese leaves.

Part of the Chinese language's fondness for classifying things into groups can be seen in the way the names of foods work – if you know that *huáng guā* is a cucumber (*huáng* means 'yellow') and that *Hāmì guā* is a melon from the town of Hami, it doesn't take much to realise that *guā* is the word used to classify fruit and vegetables with a high water content.

5 ***Wǒ yào*** I want

Though there are, of course, other ways to say 'I'd like', it is not impolite to say *wǒ yào* ('I want') as it might be in English. To refuse something, you can say *wǒ bù yào* – add *xiè xie nǐ* if you like.

6 **Numbers**

A complete list of numbers can be found at the back of the book. Note: There are two words for 'two' in Chinese. *Èr* is used in counting and in compound numbers (forty-two etc.) and *liǎng* is used for two of anything, in the sense of 'a couple of' – e.g. *liǎng bēi* 'two glasses'.

7 ***Píng*** and other measure words

Measure words are very important in Chinese – there are over 50 of them. They show the category to which nouns belong. *Yī píng* ('one bottle') is an obvious enough measure word. Less obvious to the speaker of English are measure words like *běn*, a volume, as in *wǒ yào yī běn shū*, 'I want one (volume of a) book', or *zhāng*, a flat paper thing, as in *wǒ yào yī zhāng piào*, 'I want a (flat paper thing) ticket'. The universal measure word *ge* gets the struggling learner of Chinese out of difficulty: *Wǒ yào wǔ ge*, 'I want five (of them)' is always understood. It is always preferable to put *ge* after a number, even if it is not strictly correct, than to use no measure word at all. Here is a list of some useful measure words:

yī ***wǎn*** *(mǐfàn)* a *bowl* (of rice)
yī ***bēi*** (chá) a *cup*, or *glass* (of tea)
liǎng ***fèn*** (bào) two *copies* (of newspapers)
wǔ ***zhī*** *(bǐ)* five pens (zhī is used for small things

like cigarettes)
yī ***shuāng*** *(kuàizi) a pair* (of chopsticks)

Remember that measure words are always used when you are being specific about 'that book' or 'five tickets'. When you are talking about things in general (e.g. 'there are a lot of bikes in Beijing' or 'I like apples'), there is no measure word and, of course, no equivalent to 'a', 'an', 'the', 'some' or 'any'.

8 ***Hái yào ma?*** Do you want anything else?

Hái is used variously to mean 'again', 'some more', 'anything else'. Here are some examples:

Hái yào píjiǔ. (I/he/we/they) would like some beer too. (The pronoun – I/he/we/they – is understood from the context.)
Hái yào píjiǔ ma? Do you want any more beer?
Hái yǒu mǐfàn. There's some rice left.
Hái yǒu qīngcài ma? Are there any more vegetables?
Hái yǒu shénme? What else is there?
Hái yǒu liǎng ge. There are two others as well.

Additional words and phrases

qīngcài green vegetables
píjiǔ beer
pútaojiǔ wine
xiáojie waitress/mademoiselle
yě also
hǎo, hǎode good, certainly
hé and, with
yī fèn yú a portion of fish
chá tea
hóng chá black (literally, red) tea (like English tea)
lù chá green tea (the sort of tea traditionally served in Chinese restaurants)
bēi cup, glass
kāfēi coffee
Kělè Coca-Cola
miàntiáo noodles
jiǎozi dumplings (filled with pork and/or vegetables)
kuàizi chopsticks
jiǔ alcohol

zhèr here
hái still, also, some more
mǐfàn rice
hěn very

Exercises

1 Listen to the cassette. You will hear Xiao Liu asking for various things. As you listen, place a tick or a cross in the box, according to whether the waiter says something is or isn't available.

(a) Fish ☐
(b) Qingdao beer ☐
(c) Vegetables ☐
(d) Rice ☐
(e) Noodles ☐
(f) Coca-Cola ☐
(g) Dumplings ☐
(h) Shanghai beer ☐

2 Listening practice

Listen to the cassette. Match the Chinese sentence you hear with its English equivalent – write the number in the box.

(a) I'd like some more beer ☐
(b) We don't want any rice ☐
(c) Please bring me some chopsticks ☐
(d) Is there any green tea? ☐
(e) She wants a cup of coffee ☐
(f) There's no fish left ☐
(g) Are there any more dumplings? ☐
(h) Two more bowls of rice ☐

3 Ordering another one of something

Hái yào shénme? What else would you like?
You can use *hái yào* to order another one of something:
MODEL: *Xiáojie, duì bù qǐ – hái yào yī píng píjiǔ?*
Excuse me please miss, can I have another bottle of beer?

Write down your answers to the following questions and then check them on the cassette.

(a) another bottle of Qingdao beer
(b) another cup of coffee
(c) another pair of chopsticks
(d) another cup of tea
(e) two more bowls of noodles
(f) three more coffees

4 Change these statements into questions and then into negatives – listen to the cassette to check your answers.

(a) Tā shì Zhōngguórén.
(b) Tā yào sì bēi chá.
(c) Píjiǔ yǒu.
(d) Tāmen shì Shànghǎirén.
(e) Nǐmen yào sān bēi kāfēi.
(f) Wǒmen yào sān píng Shànghǎi píjiǔ.
(g) Yǒu mǐfàn.

5 Rearrange this dialogue between the waiter and two customers. The customers start talking first.

Customers	*Waiter*
(1) Hǎo. Wǒmen hái yào qīngcài.	(a) Qīngcài, yú, miàntiáo, Kělè. Hǎode.
(2) Liǎng wǎn miàntiáo . . . yǒu yú ma?	(b) Yú yǒu – jīntiān hěn hǎo.**
(3) Hǎode.	(c) Nǐmen hǎo! Qǐng děng yī xiàr.
(4) Xiè xie nǐ. Qǐng gěi wǒmen liǎng píng píjiǔ.	(d) Yǒude. Hái yào shénme?
(5) Nǐ hǎo, xiānsheng.	(e) Duì bù qǐ, píjiǔ méiyǒu le.
(6) Méiyǒu! Yǒu Kělè ma?	(f) Qǐng zùo zhèr.

** jīntiān hěn hǎo – it's very good today

6 Translate into Chinese:

(1) I'd like two bottles of beer please, also, another two cups of coffee.

(2) She isn't Chinese, she's an overseas Chinese from America.

(3) There's no rice left and we've run out of noodles too.

(4) I don't want alcohol. I want a cup of tea please.

(5) Little friend, do you want a bottle of Coca-Cola?

(6) Is there any fish left?

(7) Please wait a moment.

(8) Please sit down.

Worth knowing

Eating and drinking in China

There are hundreds of restaurants in every major city, and in smaller towns the range is supplemented by street markets where cheap and tasty snacks are available. People are fiercely loyal to their own regional delights and dismissive of the food enjoyed by other regions. The people of Sichuan and Hunan love hot, spicy things, lavishly garnished with chillies. Yet another cuisine awaits visitors to northwest China (Xinjiang) where the majority of the people are Turkic and kebabs, salads, yoghurt and pitta bread are standard fare. The northerner likes wheat-based dishes and often dislikes spicy ones, and as for the Cantonese, famous for their exotic menus which include dog, cat, armadillo, snake and guinea pigs, the northerner says of them – 'They eat anything that flies, bar aeroplanes, and anything with four legs except a table.'

Prices range from ridiculously cheap to absurdly expensive. Some restaurants try to shunt foreigners off to special sections where prices are four or five times higher than ordinary Chinese will be paying the other side of the screen: it is quite in order politely to refuse, and just to wait for a table like the Chinese do. You may long occasionally for a hamburger or a cup of real coffee and there are now hotels in most big cities where you can indulge these desires. In Peking and Canton, there are even hotels selling cheese and croissants.

Hygiene may be a problem if you go to some of the cheaper restaurants – hepatitis is common in China, and hot water and soap for washing up are scarce commodities. Many Chinese carry their own chopsticks and spoon, and their own cup – certainly worth doing if you are travelling around. In big hotels you do not have to worry. The food itself is unlikely to cause problems as it is cooked fast at very high temperatures and consumed immediately. Drinking water *(kāishuǐ)* is always boiled. The Chinese often drink hot, boiled water *(rè kāishuǐ)* which is very effective in soothing the sore throats caused by the dry, dusty cold of a Northern Chinese winter.

Some regional beers (more like lager) are very good; many Chinese wines are not, and *máotái,* the strong spirit in which copious toasts are drunk at banquets, is also an acquired taste. One wine which the visitor should try to sample is from Shaoxing, an ancient and beautiful town near Shanghai. The region is full of lakes and has a cool, damp climate not dissimilar from Britain's: the local wine *(Shàoxīng jiǔ)* is drunk hot, probably as an antidote to the damp air, and tastes like sherry.

Waiters and waitresses do not get tips in China, but nevertheless service is reasonable considering how desperately crowded the restaurants can be; in places where few foreigners are seen, the mixture of curiosity and natural Chinese courtesy towards 'foreign guests' will ensure plenty of attention.

3 Getting about in town

Key words and expressions

dōng	east
nán	south
xī	west
běi	north
wàng běi zǒu	go north
Běijīng Fàndiàn zài nǎr?	Where's the Peking Hotel?
Duō shǎo qían?	How much (money)?
Bù xíng!	It's not allowed!
Yuǎn ma?	Is it far?
Qù Běijīng Fàndiàn zuǒ nǎ lù gōng gòng qì chē?	To go to the Peking Hotel, which bus do I take?
Jiù daò le	Then you'll be there

Conversations

1 Jenny Lo asks directions to Tienanmen.

JENNY: Nǐ hǎo – duì bù qǐ, Tiēnānmén zài nǎr?[1]
XU: Tiēnānmén: wàng běi zǒu,[2] jiù dào le.
JENNY: Xiè xie nǐ. Tiēnānmén yuǎn ma?[3]
XU: Bù yuǎn.
JENNY: Xiè xie.
XU: Bù xiè.[4]

2 In the China Arts and Crafts Shop Jenny Lo is buying a teapot and a teacup.

JENNY: Xiānsheng! Xiānsheng!
MAN: Nǐ hǎo!
JENNY: Nǐ hǎo – kěyǐ kàn kan zhè ge chá hú ma?

MAN: Zhè ge ma?
JENNY: Bù – bù yào zhè ge. Kěyǐ kàn kan nà ge chá hú ma?
MAN: Ah, duì bù qǐ. Zhè ge ma . . . ?
JENNY: Zhè ge hěn hǎo. Duō shǎo qián?
MAN: Zhè ge . . . Wǔ kuài liù máo qián[5].
JENNY: Hǎode. Wǒ hái yào kàn kan[6] chá bēi – yǒu ma?
MAN: Yǒude – děng yī xiàr . . . Nǐ kàn zhè ge ba.
JENNY: Zhè ge chá bēi hěn hǎo. Duō shǎo qián . . . ?
MAN: Zhè ge . . . zhè ge sān kuài wǔ.
JENNY: Hǎo . . . yí gòng duō shǎo qián?
MAN: Jiǔ kuài yī máo qían . . . duì bù qǐ, rénmínbì bù xíng. Qǐng nǐ gěi wǒ waìhùi . . . xiè xie nǐ.
JENNY: Xiè xie – zài jiàn.

3 Jenny asks which bus to take to the Friendship Store and where the bus stop is.

JENNY: Xiānsheng! Duì bù qǐ, Yǒuyì Shāngdiàn zài nàr?
MAN: Wàng nán zǒu, jiù dàole.
JENNY: Yuǎn ma?
MAN: Hěn yuǎn . . . 40 fēnzhōng . . .
JENNY: Aaa . . . qù[7] Yǒuyì Shāngdiàn, zǔo nǎ lù gōng gòng qì chē?
MAN: Yī lù . . . hái yǒu sì lù.
JENNY: Yī lù, sì lù . . . xiè xie nǐ. Gōng gòng qì chē zhàn zài nǎr?
MAN: Nǐ kàn . . . [He points: she is standing next to it.]

Explanations

1 ***Zài nǎr*** Where is/are?

The verb *zài,* 'to be present' or 'to be located at', is very useful:
Tiēnānmén zài nǎr? Where is Tienanmen Square?
Zài nǎr mǎi piào? Where can I buy a ticket?

Note: When you are asking where a place is, the word order is: name of place + *zài năr.* When you are asking where you can do something, the word order is: *zài năr* + action.

Lăo Wang zài ma? Is Lao Wang there? (used especially when phoning)
Lăo Wang bù zài. (No) Lao Wang isn't there/here
Nĭ jīa zài năr? Where is your home?
Wŏ jīa zài Shànghăi My home is in Shanghai
Tā zài zhèr She/he is here

2 The compass points

In giving directions, Chinese people often say 'go north' or 'go west' rather than 'turn left' or 'turn right'. They have a very good sense of direction: you may not know where north is, but they will!

The Chinese list their compass points in a different order from us:
East-South-West-North *dōng-nán-xī-bĕi*

They also express south-east, north-east etc. differently:
south-east *dōngnán* (literally, east-south)
north-east *dōngbĕi* (literally, east-north)
south-west *xīnán* (literally, west-south)
north-west *xībĕi* (literally, west-north)

Zhōng ('central' was traditionally the fifth compass point and occurs in many place names – e.g. *Zhōngguó* (China) – the Central Country or Middle Kingdom.

Compass points also figure widely in Chinese culture as, for example, in the well-known song *Dōng Fāng Hóng. (Fāng* means 'from the direction of' and *hóng* – red.) Translated into English as 'The East is Red', this song was widely sung when Mao Ze Dong was in power.

Similarly, in China you are either a *bĕifāngrén* (a person from the north, a northerner) or a *nánfāngrén* (southerner).

3 *Yuǎn* To be far away

Gùgōng hěn yuǎn The Forbidden City is a long way (from here)
Běijīng Fàndiàn yuǎn ma? Is it far to the Peking Hotel?
Wanfujing bù yuǎn Wanfujing is not far

4 *Bù xiè* You're welcome
Bù xiè literally means 'Don't thank (me)' and is one way of saying 'you're welcome'. You can also say *bù kèqi,* which literally means 'don't be polite'. (*Kèqi* sounds similar to the English word 'courtesy', which makes it easy to remember.)

5 Money, money, money

The basic unit of currency is the *yuán*. It is divided into 100 *fēn.* The word *kuài* is used in speech for *yuán.*

1 yuán/kuài	=	100 fēn
10 fēn	=	1 máo (written yī jiǎo, on bank notes)
10 máo	=	1 yuán/kuài

When expressing sums of money, the word *qián* ('money') is often put after the sum, though people don't always bother.

Wǔ kuài qián Five kuai (money)
Wǔ kuài, liù máo qián Five kuai, six mao (money)
Wǔ kuài, liù Five kuai six (*máo* is understood, *qián* is dropped)
Bā kuài wǔ máo sān Eight kuai, five mao, three (*fēn* is understood)

To express a sum such as 'two kuai, three fen' where there are no *máo,* the word *líng* (zero) is used:
Jiǔ kuài líng wǔ fēn qián Nine kuai, zero mao, five fen

Remember to use the word *liǎng* for 'two': *liǎng máo, liǎng fēn, liǎng kuài.* The word *èr* is only used when counting 1-2-3-4 etc.

If all this seems very complicated, don't worry – the standard of honesty when dealing with 'foreign friends' is very high in China, and if you offer what you think is the right sum, it will be a matter of pride for most Chinese not to cheat you.

6 *Kàn kan* To have a look

This doubling up of verbs to 'soften' the effect of what is said is a common feature in spoken Chinese. Sometimes, just to ease pronunciation, *yi* goes between the words: *kàn kan* or *kàn yi kàn* – 'to have a look'. The sense is that the speaker is sorry to be a nuisance. Other examples often heard are:

děng	to wait	*děng yi děng*	to wait a little
shuō	to speak	*shuō yi shuō*	to have a word with someone (on someone else's behalf)
xiǎng	to think	*xiǎng yi xiǎng*	to think it over

N.B. When there is no *yi* between the two words, the second half of the phrase is unstressed.

7 *Qù* To go

You can say:
Wǒ qù Zhōngguó I'm going to China
Lǎo Wang shénme shíhou qù Yīngguó? When is Lao Wang going to England?

Or:

Wǒ dào Zhōngguó qù I'm going to China
Lǎo Wang shénme shíhou dào Yīngguó qù? When is Lao Wang going to England?

Useful place names

gōng yuán	park
dàjīe	avenue
lù	road
shān	mountain/hill
hǎi	sea
hú	lake
gōng	palace
tán	temple (Taoist)
miào	temple (Buddhist)
shìchǎng	market
mén	gate
líng	tomb
fàndiàn	hotel
bīnguǎn	hotel ('guesthouse')
Yǒuyì Shāngdiàn	Friendship Store

Additional words and phrases

Gùgōng	the Forbidden City (in Beijing)
Tiāntán	the Temple of Heaven (in Beijing)
Tiān an mén	the Gate of Heavenly Peace (in Beijing)
zài jiàn	goodbye
qù	to go
hěn hǎo	very good
yī zhāng piào	ticket (*zhang*: measure word)
chá hú	teapot
chá bēi	teacup
kàn kan/kàn yi kàn	to have a look
yígòng	altogether
jiā	home (family)
dà	big
bù xiè! / *bù kèqì!*	you're welcome!
chū zū qì chē	taxi
zì xíng chē	bicycle
gōng gòng qì chē	bus
gōng gòng qì chē zhàn	bus stop
23 – lù	number 23
zài zhèr	it's here
nà ge	that, those one(s)
zhè ge	this, these one(s)
huā píng	vase ('flower bottle')
mǎi	buy
shí jiān	time
nǎ lù?	which one (for a bus)?

Exercises

1 Using *zài*

Listen to the cassette. Practise the sentences and then translate them into English.

(a) Gùgōng zài nǎr?

(b) Xiǎo Liu zài ma?

(c) Nǐ jīa zài nǎr?

(d) Jenny zài Běijīng ma?

(e) Tāmen bù zài Shànghǎi.

(f) Zài nǎr mǎi huā píng?

2 Buying things

Re-arrange these sentences in the right order. The customer speaks first.

Customer	*Shopgirl*
(1) Duō shao qián?	(a) Xiè xie nǐ. Zài jiàn.
(2) Xiǎojie!	(b) Bù xíng. Qǐng gěi wǒ wàihùi.
(3) Qǐng gěi wǒ kàn yi kàn zhè ge chá hú.	(c) 10 kuài 5 máo qián.
(4) Hǎo, wǒ mǎi zhè ge. Rénmínbì xíng ma?	(d) Nǐ hǎo. Yào shénme?
(5) Hǎode, hǎode	(e) Kěyǐ. Zhè ge hěn hǎo.

3 Place names.

Match these to their English equivalents.

(a) Zhōng nán hǎi	(1) Nanjing East Street (Shanghai's main shopping street)
(b) Nánjīng dōng lù	(2) West Lake (Hangzhou)
(c) Běijīng dōng lù	(3) Northsea Park (Beijing)
(d) Xī hú	(4) Central and Southern Lakes (Beijing – the 10 Downing Street of China)

(e) Zhōng shān gōng yuán	(5) Beijing East Street (Nanjing)
(f) Dōng líng	(6) Central Hill Park (Beijing)
(g) Běihǎi gōng yuán	(7) East Peace Gate Avenue (Beijing)
(h) Dōngānmén dàjīe	(8) Eastern tombs (near Shenyang)

4 Listen to the cassette and fill in the gaps in the dialogue:

JENNY: Xiānsheng! Duì bù qǐ, (i)_____ _____ zài nǎr?

MAN: (ii)_____ _____? Wàng (iii)_____ zǒu, jiù dào le.

JENNY: Yuǎn ma?

MAN: (iv)_____ _____

JENNY: Qù (v)_____ _____ zùo nǎ lù (vi)_____ _____ qì chē?

MAN: (vii)_____ lù.

JENNY: (viii)_____ _____ qì chē zhàn zài nǎr?

MAN: Nǐ kàn!

JENNY: Ah! Xiè xie nǐ.

5 Asking which bus to take

Listen to the cassette. Ask the question and substitute different place names each time for the one which is underlined.

MODEL: Qù Wanfujing zǒu nǎ lù gōng gòng qì chē?

Substitute:

(1) Nánjīng dōng lù
(2) Zhōng shān lù
(3) Běihǎi gōng yuán
(4) Tiān ān mén
(5) Dōng fāng shìchǎng

6 Asking the price of things

(a) Ask the price of each article

(b) Give the price in two ways

e.g.: (i) ¥ 3.30 Sān kuài sān máo qián
(ii) ¥ 3.30 Sān kuài sān

A

B

C

D

(c) Check your answers by listening to the cassette.

Note: The numbers 1 – 1,000,000 are listed at the end of the book.

7 Chinese consequences!

You get into a taxi. Choose the most likely thing you would say to the driver and his most likely answer. Compare your version with the cassette.

(1) YOU: (a) Nǐ hǎo. Wǒ qù Wanfujing.
(b) Zaì jiàn. Wǒ dào Shànghǎi qù.

(2) DRIVER: (a) Rénmínbì bù xíng.
(b) Hǎo.

(3) YOU: (a)Nǐ shì Běijīngrén ma?
(b)Nǐ shì Měiguórén ma?

(4) DRIVER: (a) Bù. Wǒ shì Tiānjīnrén.
(b) Wǒ dào Měiguó qù.

(5) YOU: (a) Wanfujing yuǎn ma?
(b) Gōng gòng qì chē zhàn zài nǎr?

(6) DRIVER: (a) Wanfujing hěn yuǎn . . . Běijīng hǎo ma?
(b) Wanfujing zài Běijīng. Běijīng zài Zhōngguó.

(7) YOU: (a) Běijīng hěn hǎo.
(b) Dàjīa hǎo.

8 Extra practice

(1) You're asking directions. Ask:
(a) Where's the Dongfang Hotel? (b) Is it far?

(2) You meet someone for the first time. Ask:
(a) Is your home in Beijing? (b) Is your home far?
(c) Are you a northerner?

(3) You're in a shop. Ask:
(a) Can I see that vase? (b) How much does it cost?

(4) You're in the street. Ask:
(a) Which bus do I get to the Forbidden City? (b) Where is the bus stop?

(5) You're in the bus. Ask:
(a) Is the Forbidden City far? (b) How much does the ticket cost?

9 Practise the numbers 1-100

Worth knowing

Shopping in China

Most foreign visitors to China change their own currency into so-called Foreign Exchange Certificates (FEC) which they use to pay for goods and services. These are called *wàihùi* in Chinese. Ordinary Chinese citizens use *rénmínbì* (people's currency) which are, in theory, exchangeable one for one with FEC. In practice, FEC are rather more desirable than *rénmínbì* as they can be used to buy imported goods, such as cassette recorders, which are both scarce and more expensive when purchased with *rénmínbì.* So there is now a black market in currency dealing. It flourishes especially in Canton, with its close proximity to Hong Kong. But getting large bundles of *rénmínbì* on the cheap is not much use, as they will not be accepted in most places – and anyway, it is illegal.

Most shops in China are open seven days a week, from 9 a.m. to 8 p.m. Sunday is the busiest day. There are many department stores, as well as specialised shops which sell books, records, clothes, shoes and so on. There are also Friendship Stores *(Yǒuyì Shāngdiàn)* and antique shops which take only FEC and cater almost exclusively to foreigners and overseas Chinese. These sell high-class souvenirs, jewellery, medicines for every imaginable ailment and things which are of more use to long-term residents than to tourists, such as bicycles and sewing machines. Many big hotels have little shopping arcades – look out for silk lingerie, hand-made silk flowers, cloisonné, jade, hand-painted fans, and very reasonably priced illustrated books. All prices are fixed, as these are state shops.

'Free markets', where peasants can bring their own produce and sell it for private profit, are wonderful places to wander, to have a snack – a bowl of noodles with hot pepper sauce, guaranteed to bring tears to your eyes – and to buy some fresh fruit to supplement the package tour diet. The bigger ones often sell antiques, clothes, flowers, caged birds and traditional medicines. Bargaining is very much in order for antiques, but the prices quoted for fruit, snacks and bread are normally the same as the ones the local Chinese are paying – and very cheap!

4 A trip to Xian

Key expressions

Huǒchē zhàn zài nǎr?	Where's the railway station?
Zài nǎr mǎi piào?	Where can I buy a ticket?
Wǒ yào mǎi yī zhāng piào	I want to buy a ticket (*zhang*: measure word for flat objects)
Shénme shíhou yào qù Xīan?	When do you want to go to Xian? (*shénme shíhou:* literally, 'what period', when)
Xīngqī sān shì wǒmende chūnjié	Wednesday is (our) Spring Festival
Nǐ yào mǎi jǐ zhāng?	How many (tickets) do you want to buy?
yìngzuò	hard seats
yìngwò/yìngxí	hard sleepers
ruǎnwò/ruǎnxí	soft sleepers
Huǒchē jǐ diǎn kāi?	What time does the train leave?
Shàngwǔ jiǔ diǎn	Nine a.m.
Xiàwǔ, liǎng diǎn	Two p.m.
Qù Guǎngzhōude huǒchē jǐ diǎn kāi?	What time does the train for Guangzhou (Canton) leave?
Huǒchē jǐ diǎn dào Xīan?	What time does the train get to Xian?

Conversations

Jenny Lo is trying to find the station

JENNY: Duì bù qǐ, huǒchē zhàn zài nàr?
WANG: Huǒchē zhàn . . . wàng běi zǒu, jiù dào le.
JENNY: Yuǎn ma?
WANG: Bù yuǎn. Shí fēnzhōng.
JENNY: Hǎo, xiè xie nǐ.
WANG: Bù xiè.

Jenny Lo is buying a train ticket at the station

JENNY: Nǐ hǎo. Wǒ yào mǎi yī zhāng piào.
LIU: Nǐ yào qù nǎr?
JENNY: Dào Xīan qù.
LIU: Shénme shíhou yào qù?
JENNY: Xīngqī yī. Kěyǐ ma?
LIU: Nǐ děng yī xiàr, hǎo ma, wǒ kàn yi kàn. Ah, duì bù qǐ, xīngqī yī méiyǒu piào. Nǐ zhīdào, xīngqī sān shì wǒmende[1] chūnjié.[2] Mǎi piào hěn bù róngyì.[3]
JENNY: Ah . . . na, xīngqī sì kěyǐ ma? Yǒu piào ma?
LIU: Xīngqī sī . . . nǐ děng yi děng . . . (Shuffles papers) Hǎo, xīngqī sì, yǒu piào. Nǐ yào mǎi jǐ zhāng?
JENNY: Mǎi yī zhāng. Dūo shǎo qián?
LIU: Gěi wǒ 70 kuài qián.

Jenny has paid for her ticket and asks what time the train leaves

JENNY: Gěi nǐ 70 kuài qián. Hǔochē jǐ diǎn kāi?[4]
LIU: Xīngqī sì, xiàwǔ, sān diǎn.
JENNY: Jǐ diǎn dào Xīan?[4]
LIU: Xīngqī wǔ, xiàwǔ, sì diǎn dào Xīan.
JENNY: Shíjīan hěn cháng . . .
LIU: Na . . . Zhōngguó hěn dà!

Explanations

1 *Wŏmende chūnjié* Our Spring Festival

To form words like 'my', 'mine', 'your', 'yours' etc. add *de,* the possessive particle, to the pronouns 'I', 'you' etc:

wŏde	my, mine	*wŏmende*	our, ours
nĭde	your, yours	*nĭmende*	your, yours
tāde	his/her/hers/its	*tāmende*	their, theirs

Unit 5 goes into the use of *de* in more detail. Here is another example of the use of *de:*

Qù Shànghăide huŏchē jĭ diăn kāi? What time does the (going to) Shanghai train leave?

Qù Tiānānménde gōng gòng qì chē zhàn zài năr? Where's the bus stop for the Tiananmen bus?

Qù Bĕijīngde fēijī jĭ diăn qĭ fēi? What times does the Beijing plane take off?

2 *Chūnjié*

Chūnjié is the Spring Festival, or Chinese New Year. The Chinese used to use the lunar calendar and *chūnjié* marks the end of the old lunar year. Although the Gregorian calendar is now used in China, the old festivals are still fixed according to the lunar calendar. There is a public holiday on 1 January, but *chūnjié* is the real festival and is similar to Christmas in the West – families get together, eat and drink, and everything stops for a week! There are fireworks and processions in rural districts and in the south, where the weather feels more spring-like than it does in the still frozen north.

3 *Măi piào hĕn bù róngyì*

Literally, this means 'to buy tickets is very not easy'. In English, of course, we would say 'buying', but in Chinese the verb form does not change:

Shuō pŭtōnghuà hĕn róngyì Speaking Chinese is very easy

Xiě hànze hěn bù róngyì Writing Chinese characters is very difficult
Zùo huǒchē dào Zhōngguó qù yaò duō shǎo tiān? Going to China by train requires how many days?

4 Telling the time

(Huǒchē) jǐ diǎn kāi? What time does (the train) leave?
(Huǒchē) jǐ diǎn dào Xīan? What time does (the train) get to Xian?
Xiànzài jǐ diǎn le? What time is it now?

Divisions of the day

yī fēnzhōng one minute
yī (ge) xiǎoshí one hour
yī kè one quarter (of an hour)
bàn xiǎoshí one half (of an hour)

Examples:

1 o'clock	*yī diǎn* (literally, 'one hour')
2.05	*liǎng diǎn wǔ fēn*
3.15	*sān diǎn shí wǔ fēn* or *sān diǎn yī kè*
4.25	*sì diǎn èr shí wǔ fēn*
8.30	*bā diǎn sān shí fēn* or *bā diǎn bàn*
12.55	*shí èr diǎn wǔ shí wǔ fēn*

To express the number of minutes to the hour, use *chà*

2.45	*chà yī kè sān diǎn* (literally, it lacks one quarter [to] three hours/o'clock) *sān diǎn chà yī kè* (three hours/o'clock less one quarter)
9.50	*chà shí fēn shí diǎn* (it lacks 10 minutes [to] 10 o'clock) *shí diǎn chà shí fēn* (10 o'clock less 10 minutes) *jiǔ diǎn wǔ shí fēn* (9 hours 50 minutes)

To specify a.m./p.m.

Chinese does not use the 24-hour clock in speech, and specifying whether you mean morning, afternoon, evening or night-time is more complicated than it is in English. Of course, as in English, if it is clear from the context what time of day you are referring to, you don't need to specify. But if you do, here's how to do it:

zǎoshàng is used from about 0400 to 0700 (*zǎo* means 'early'; *shàng* means 'above'):
0600 *zǎoshàng liù diǎn* (early morning, six hours)

shàngwǔ is used from about 0800 to 1200 (*shàng* means 'above'; *wǔ* means 'noon'):
0910 *shàngwǔ jiǔ diǎn shí fēn*

zhōngwǔ is used from about 1200 to 1300 (*zhōng* means 'middle'; *wǔ* means 'noon'):
1215 *zhōngwǔ shí èr diǎn shí wǔ fēn* or *shí èr diǎn yī kè*

xiàwǔ is used from about 1300 to 1800 (*xià* means 'below'; *wú* means 'noon'):
1515 *xiàwǔ sān diǎn yī kè* or *sān diǎn shí wǔ fēn*

wǎnshàng may be used from about 1900 to 2400 (*wǎn* means 'late'; *shàng* means 'above'):
2030 *wǎnshàng bā diǎn bàn*

Sometimes the word *zhěng,* meaning 'exactly', is attached to clock hours:
Fēijī liǎng diǎn zhěng qǐ fēi The plane takes off at 2 o'clock exactly

Additional words and phrases

fēnzhōng	minute(s)
fēijī	aeroplane
fēijī chǎng	airport (literally 'aeroplane' field)
nǐ zhīdào	you know
chūnjié	Chinese New Year (Spring Festival)
(bù) róngyì	(not) easy
wǒmende	our
shíjiān	time
(hěn) cháng	(very) long
(hěn) dà	(very) big
háishi	or, either
qǐ fēi	take off (aeroplanes)
hǎo ma?	is that O.K.?/do you agree?

Days of the week

Learn the numbers 1-6 and you've nearly learnt the days of the week in Chinese. Only Sunday is different.

xīngqī yī Monday (First day of the week)
xīngqī èr Tuesday (Second day of the week)
xīngqī sān Wednesday (Third day of the week)
xīngqī sì Thursday (Fourth day of the week)
xīngqī wǔ Friday (Fifth day of the week)
xīngqī liù Saturday (Sixth day of the week)
xīngqī tiān } Sunday (day off. Traditionally *tiān*
xīngqī rì } means 'heaven' and *rì* means 'sun')

Other expressions of time

yī tiān one day
yī ge xīngqī one week
yī ge yuè one month
yī nián one year
jīntiān today
zuótiān yesterday
míngtiān tomorrow
hòu tiān the day after tomorrow
shàng ge xīngqī last week
xià ge xīngqī next week
qù nián last year
míng nián next year
jià rì holiday

Months

Learn the numbers 1-12, plus the word *yuè* ('month'), and you've learnt the names of all the months

yī yuè	January	*qī yuè*	July
èr yuè	February	*bā yuè*	August
sān yuè	March	*jiǔ yuè*	September
sì yuè	April	*shí yuè*	October
wǔ yuè	May	*shí yī yuè*	November
liù yuè	June	*shí èr yuè*	December

Years

Simply list the numbers and add *nián* ('year'):

1966 – *yī jiŭ liù liù nián* ('one nine six six year')
1789 – *yī qī bā jiŭ nián* ('one seven eight nine year')

Dates

The Chinese order is year – month – day.
The word *hào,* 'number', corresponds to our 2nd, 3rd, 4th etc. for dates.

1st October 1949 – *Yī jiŭ sì jiŭ nián shí yuè yī hào.*
9th September 1976 – *Yī jiŭ qī liù nián jiŭ yuè jiŭ hào.*

Exercises

1 Train times

Look at the departures board. Listen to the announcements on the cassette. Fill in what time each train leaves.

	Destination	*Departure Time*
A.	Shanghai	
B.	Tianjin	
C.	Turfan	
D.	Guangzhou	
E.	Beijing	

2 Aeroplane departures and arrivals

MODEL:

PASSENGER: *Qù Guăngzhōude fēijī jĭ diăn qĭ fēi?*
What time does the Guangzhou (Canton) plane take off?

CAAC OFFICIAL: *Shàngwŭ bā diăn shí fēn.*
0810.

PASSENGER: *Jĭ diăn daò Guăngzhōu?*
What time does it get to Guangzhou?

CAAC OFFICIAL: *Shí yī diăn.*
1100.

Now look at the timetable and ask and answer about Fuzhou, Guangzhou, Guilin, Hong Kong, London, and Paris.

	From	*To*	*Departure*	*Arrival*
A.	Beijing	Fuzhou	0755	1040
B.	Beijing	Guangzhou	0930	1220
C.	Beijing	Guilin	1355	1645
D.	Beijing	Hong Kong*	1615	1825
E.	Beijing	London	1745	1855
F.	Beijing	Paris**	1945	0655

*In *pŭtōnghuà,* Hong Kong is *Xiāng Găng,* which means 'fragrant harbour'. This is also what the (anglicised) version of the original Cantonese name means.
**Pronounced *Bālí* in *pŭtōnghuà*
(The correct version is on the cassette.)

3 Match these English sentences with the Chinese ones you hear on the cassette.

Example: (1) Where's the railway station? ☐
(D) Huŏchē zhàn zài năr?

You put D into the box next to sentence 1.

(1) Where's the bus stop? ☐

(2) Go west, you'll get there. ☐

(3) Is it far? ☐

(4) Yes, it is very. ☐

(5) Which bus do I take to go to the railway station? ☐

(6) Number 6. ☐

(7) Where can I buy a train ticket? ☐

(8) Here. ☐

(9) I want to go to the airport. ☐

(10) What time does the Canton train leave? ☐

4 Dates

Say in Chinese:
(Remember the order: year – month – day)

(a) Your date of birth
(b) The date of the declaration of the Second World War
(c) Christmas Day
(d) The birthday of someone close to you
(e) The year the First World War ended

5 Here is the itinerary for your tour round China. Some parts have not been filled in. Listen to the tape and fill in the rest.

Place	*Means of Transport*	*Arrive*	*Sight-seeing*	*Hotel*
Beijing				
Xian		3.30 p.m. Wednesday	Terracotta Army	
Turfan			Dunhuang Grottoes	
Urumqi	Train from Turfan			
Kunming				Kunming Hotel
Hong Kong				

6 Take the passenger's part in this conversation at the railway station. Then listen to the cassette to check your answers.

YOU:	(Hullo. I want a ticket to Xian.)
CLERK:	Hǎode. Shénme shíhòu qù Xīan?
YOU:	(Are there any tickets for Wednesday?)
CLERK:	Děng yī xiàr . . . duì bù qǐ, méiyǒu.
YOU:	(How about Friday?)
CLERK:	Wǒ kàn yi kàn, hǎo ma . . . yǒude.
YOU:	(Good! Can I have four please?)
CLERK:	Yào ruǎnxí háishi yìngxí?
YOU:	(Soft sleeper please.)
CLERK:	Hǎode . . . qǐng gěi wǒ 420 kuài.
YOU:	(Do you take renminbi?)
CLERK:	Duì bù qǐ – bù xíng. Qǐng gěi wǒ wàihuì.
YOU:	(Here's 420 kuai. What time does the train leave?)
CLERK:	Xīngqī èr wǎnshàng qī diǎn.
YOU:	(And when does it get there?)
CLERK:	Xīngqī sān wǎnshàng bā diǎn sì shí wǔ fēn.

Worth Knowing

Long-distance travel in China

Travel by train in China is a wonderful experience, giving you a chance to meet the Chinese in a very free and easy way. Chinese passengers will welcome the diversion of a foreigner to chat to on a long journey: as well as giving you the chance to practise your Chinese, many of them will be eager to practise their English. Travel in *yìngxí* or *yìngwò* (second class, or 'hard sleeper') is probably best for this as in third class, *yìngzuò* ('hard seat'), the seats consist of hard wooden benches, crammed with people and chickens, full of noise and cigarette smoke, and best used only for short journeys. The passengers in *yìngxí* tend to be middle-management level rather than peasants; so their Chinese is easier to understand and there will be a few who speak English who can help things along. These carriages, too, are smoke-filled as there are no 'No Smoking' compartments on Chinese trains – but you do get a better class of cigarette! If you travel *ruǎnxí* ('soft sleeper' or first class), you will get a spotlessly clean compartment for four people, with comfortable, European-style couchettes, and little lace antimacassars on the head-rests.

There is always a restaurant car on Chinese trains, and the food can be surprisingly good considering the cramped conditions in which the cooking is done. However, hygiene is not so good, and you should carry your own chopsticks, cup, spoon and bowl to be on the safe side. A few extra snacks for long journeys (e.g. the 4-day marathon across the Gobi Desert from Beijing) will not come amiss, though at every station the train stops and people rush onto the platform to buy whatever food is sold there: it can vary from delicious regional specialities to rather unpleasant dry biscuits.

Buying tickets for train journeys is best done at an office of Luxingshe, the Chinese state tourist organisation: however, they are not always as efficient as they could be and in many places you will have to go to the railway station where, particularly as public holidays approach, the queue for tickets can make a rugby scrum look like a tea party.

There are different classes of train, and you pay a supplement for faster trains. The different classes are:
tè kuài chē (express – like the one that connects Guangzhou to Beijing and is a good route up from Hong Kong)
kuài chē (fast train – most long-distance trains are in this class)
màn chē (slow train – usually a local train which stops at small villages)

Long-distance buses serve destinations in the south of China, and many start from Hong Kong or Macao, which makes it easy to find out information about them.

The Chinese state airline is CAAC which, in recent years, has been modernising rapidly, buying new planes, computerising ticket sales and improving the training of its cabin staff. CAAC is adding more flights to the timetable all the time but the increasing prosperity and mobility of the Chinese, as well as the ever-increasing numbers of tourists and foreign business people, means that demand is constantly outstripping supply. It is still difficult to make onward bookings from your destination (unless you hand the whole thing over to Luxingshe and give them plenty of notice), so the general rule is that the moment you arrive somewhere you book your ticket out again. (This applies to trains as well.)

Boats are a wonderful way to see China – although they are not for the traveller in a hurry. Some trips are well known – the trip up the Yangtse Gorges, for example – others, such as the boat from Guilin to Guangzhou (Canton), are less so. The same rules about food and hygiene apply on board ships as on trains – in fact, rather more so as the river water is often used for washing-up and making soup. But do try to take a boat at some stage during your trip: Marco Polo's descriptions of the Grand Canal are still recognisable in the scenes of river life today.

5 In the Xian Guesthouse

Key expressions

Wǒ hěn lèi	I'm very tired
Wǒmen dàole	We've arrived
Wǒ mǎile huǒchē piào	I've bought a train ticket
Shì shéide shū? *Zhèi běn shū shì shéide?*	Whose book is this?
Yǒu fángjiān ma?	Have you got any rooms?
Yǒu yī ge hěn hǎode	There's a very good one
Yī yè duō shǎo qián?	How much per night?
Méi guānxi!	Never mind!
Wǒ dǎ suàn zhù yī xīngqī	I'll be staying one week
Shì wǒde fángjiān	It's my room
Tài gùi le!	It's too expensive!
Yǒu píenyìde ma?	Have you got a cheaper one?

Conversations

Jenny has just arrived at Xian Station and she takes a taxi to go to the hotel – the *Xīan Bīnguǎn* or Xian Guesthouse.

JENNY: Nǐ hǎo.
DRIVER: Nǐ hǎo. Dào nǎr qù?
JENNY: Wǒ yào qù Xīan Bīnguǎn.
DRIVER: Hǎo . . . Zǒuba . . . Nǐ cóng Běijīng láide ma?[1]
JENNY: Shì de. Shíjiān hěn cháng. Wǒ hěn lèi.
DRIVER: Běijīng hěn hǎo . . . Wǒ shì Běijīngrén. Wǒ māma, bāba, dōu[2] zài Běijīng.
JENNY: Shì ma?[3]

DRIVER: Hăo, wŏmen dàole. Zhè shì Xīan Bīnguăn.
JENNY: Duō shăo qían?
DRIVER: Shí kuài qián. Gĕi nĭ piào[4] . . . Zài jiàn.
JENNY: Zài jiàn.

Jenny arrives at the hotel

The first room she's offered is too expensive, but she takes a cheaper one and says she's staying a week.

JENNY: Nĭ hăo.
FU WU YUAN: Nĭ hăo.
JENNY: Yŏu fángjiān ma?
FU WU YUAN: Dĕng yi dĕng, wŏ kàn yi kàn . . . Yŏude, yī ge hĕn hăode.
JENNY: Yī yè, duō shăo qián?
FU WU YUAN: Yī yè, 150 kuài qián.
JENNY: Tài guì le!
FU WU YUAN: Bù guì!
JENNY: Yŏu piényìde ma?
FU WU YUAN: Yŏu yī ge – hĕn xiăode.
JENNY: Méi guānxi – duō shăo qián?
FU WU YUAN: Yī yè, 58 kuài qián.
JENNY: Wŏ dă suàn zhù yī xīngqī.[5]

Explanations

1 *Nĭ cóng Bĕijīng láide ma?*

Literally: 'You are a coming-from-Beijing person?' *De* is a possessive particle meaning 'having the quality of' – Jenny is a person who 'has the quality of having arrived' from Beijing. Another example of this usage is the plea from bus conductors heard over the tannoy on crowded buses in Beijing:
Méi măi piào de tóngzhìmen qĭng nĭmen măi piào!
The not-having-bought-tickets comrades, please buy tickets!

2 *Wǒ māma, bāba, dōu zài Běijīng*

'My mother and father are (all) in Beijing.' *Dōu* here means all. When the taxi driver says *dōu zài Běijīng*, he is thinking of his whole family – grandparents, parents, brothers and sisters.

If you want to be specific and say both, Chinese simply uses *liǎng ge rén* – 'two people':

Tāmen liǎng ge rén mǎi piào	They are both buying tickets
Wǒmen liǎng ge rén qù Běijīng	We're both going to Beijing

3 *Shì ma?* Is that so?

This is used in Chinese like the English 'Really?', and with an equal range of expressiveness – bored, fascinated, disbelieving, amused etc.

4 *Gěi nǐ piào*

'I give you the tickets.' Chinese taxi drivers always give you receipts for the exact amount of the fare. In theory, you do not tip them, although cigarettes are always welcome; in practice some now expect tips, and others would not refuse if offered.

5 *Dǎ suàn* To plan (to do something)

Wǒ dǎ suàn zhù yī xīngqī I'll be staying one week
Wǒ dǎ suàn zhù yī yè I'll be staying one night
Wǒ dǎ suàn zhù jǐ tiān I'll be staying several days

zhù = live, stay, inhabit:
Wǒ zhù zài Shànghǎi I live in Shanghai.

A tale of two particles – *le* and *de*

Chinese uses a few particles a great deal and these two are the most important:

Le

In this book we look at two uses of *le*. In both these cases, *le* indicates that a certain limit has been passed and a state of affairs has changed or progressed:

Fángjiān tài guì le!	The room's too expensive!
Nĭ tài hăo le!	You're wonderful (too good)!
Tiànqì tài lĕng le!	The weather's freezing (too cold)!
Jīntiān tài rè le!	It's too hot today!
(Wŏ) tài lèi le!	(I'm) too (so, very) tired!

Le may also be used to express the past tense, usually with a time reference (which may be understood rather than specified). The negative is formed by adding *méi* (cf. méiyŏu) to the verb:

chī to eat	*chīle* ate	*méi chī* didn't eat/ haven't eaten
dào to reach	*dàole* reached	*méi dào* didn't reach/ haven't reached
hē to drink	*hēle* drank	*méi hē* didn't drink/ haven't drunk
kàn to look	*kànle* looked	*méi kàn* didn't look/ haven't looked
măi to buy	*măile* bought	*méi măi* didn't buy/ haven't bought
qù to go	*qùle* went	*méi qù* didn't go/ haven't gone

Here are some examples:

Dōngxi dōu gùi le	Things have all got more expensive
Xiăo Liu lăo le!	Xiao Liu's aged!
Chī fàn le ma?	Have you eaten? (*Fàn* = 'rice'; *chī fàn* = 'to eat rice' – for obvious reasons, a synonym for 'eating')
Wŏ méi măi piào	I haven't bought a ticket

Tā méi kàn bào	She hasn't seen/read the newspaper
Wǒ hái méi chī	I haven't eaten yet
Zuótiān tā méi hē jiǔ, zhǐ hē le kāishuǐ	Yesterday he didn't drink alcohol, he just drank water

De

As we saw in unit 4, *de* can be used:

(1) To form possessive adjectives and pronouns:

*Zhè shì wǒ**de** shū*	That's my book
*Zhè zhāng piào shì tā**de***	That ticket's hers

(2) To show possession in the same way as an apostrophe 's' does in English:

*Lǎo Zhang**de** māma hěn hǎo*	Lao Zhang's mother is very nice
*Zhè shì Xiǎo Liu**de** huǒchē piào*	That's Xiao Liu's train ticket

(3) To show that somebody or something has a certain quality:

*Qù Shànghǎi**de** huǒchē jǐ diǎn kāi?*	What time does the Shanghai train leave? (literally, 'The going-to-Shanghai-train what time leaves')
*Mài bào**de** rén bù zài*	The newspaper seller isn't there (literally, 'The selling-papers-person isn't there')
*Zài Wánfujing mǎi dōngxi**de** rén hěn duō*	There are a lot of people shopping in Wanfujing (literally, 'In Wanfujing there are buying-things-people very many')
Méi mǎi piaòde tòngzhímen qǐng nǐmen mǎi piào!	Please buy tickets if you haven't already done so (literally, 'The not-having-bought-tickets-comrades please you buy tickets')

(4) It can be used to replace a noun in the same way as the English word 'one':

*Yŏu yīge hĕn hăo**de***	There's a very good one
*Zhège chá hú tài xiăole – yŏu dà**de** ma?*	This teapot's too small – have you got a bigger one?
***Dàde** shì tāde, xiăo**de** shì wŏde*	The big one's hers, the small one's mine

Family relationships

The extended family is of great importance in China, and there are different names for almost every family member.

My mother	– strictly, *wŏde māma;* in speech this is usually abbreviated to *wŏ mā.* Similarly, *wŏde bāba,* 'my father', becomes *wŏ bā.*
Brothers	– *Wŏ dìdi* – 'my younger brother' *(wŏ dì)* *Wŏ gēge* – 'my older brother' *(wŏ gē)*
Sisters	– *Wŏ jiĕjie* – 'my older sister' *(wŏ jiĕ)* *Wŏ mèimei* – 'my younger sister' *(wŏ mèi)*

People who are close friends but not actually blood relations often call each other big brother, little sister, auntie, uncle and so on.

Children	*wŏde érzi* my son *wŏde nǚér* my daughter	
Grandparents	grandmother:	*lăo lăo* or *wài pó* (maternal) *năi năi* (paternal)
	grandfather:	*lăo yé* or *wài gōng* (maternal) *yé yé* (paternal)
Marriage	husband	*wŏde zhàngfū, wŏde xiānsheng*
	wife	*wŏde tàitai, wŏde fūren*

The word *aìrén* (literally, 'loved person') can be used for husband or wife, or fiancé(e)

Examples

Lăo Zhangde aìrén tài hăole	Old Zhang's wife is wonderful
Xiăo Liude mèimei zhù zài Guăngzhōu	Young Liu's younger sister lives in Guangzhou
Wŏde péngyŏude māma shì Shànghăirén	My friend's mother is from Shanghai

Additional words and phrases

cóng	from
lái	come
dōu	all
Xīan Bīnguăn	Xian Guesthouse
jĭ tīan	several days
yī yè	one night
lĕng	cold
rè	hot
dōngxi	things
hē	drink
măi dōngxi	to go shopping (literally: to buy things)
kàn bào	to read (literally: to look at) newspaper

Exercises

1 Expressing relationships

How would you put these sentences into English?

(1) Wŏ meìmeide aìrén zuótiān măile huŏchē piào.

(2) Lăo Zhangde tàitai shì nánfāngrén.

(3) Zhè shì jīntiānde bào ma?

(4) Zhè bēi píjiŭ shì shéide?

(5) Zhè bĕn shū shì nĭde ma?

(6) Zài wŏde jiā, zhĭ yŏu liăng ge fángjiān – yīge dàde, yīge xiăode.

(7) Dàde shì nĭde, xiăode shì Lăo Wangde.

(8) Wŏ măile liăng ge chá hú – yīge guìde, yīge piényide.

2 Booking a room

Re-arrange this conversation in the right order. The *fú wù yuán* (clerk) speaks first:

Clerk	Tourist
(1) Hǎo. Huānyíng nǐmen dào Xīan Bīngǔan!	(a) Xiè xie!
(2) Yào jǐ ge fángjiān?	(b) Jǐ tiān.
(3) Nǐmen hǎo. Yào shénme?	(c) Nǐ hǎo. Wǒmen liǎng ge rén yào fángjiān.
(4) Yǒude, yǒude. Yǒu yīge hěn hǎode, yě hěn guìde; yǒu yīge xiǎode, piényide. Nǐmen dǎ suàn zhù duō shǎo shíjiān?	(d) Yào liǎng ge. Yǒu ma?

3 In each of the following sentences you can use *tài + le.* What should you say?

(1) Today's so hot!
(2) It's freezing in Beijing!
(3) You're feeling exhausted!
(4) She's wonderful!
(5) Her husband's too old!
(6) That room's too expensive!
(7) That vase is too big!
(8) This teapot's too small!

4 Talking about past tenses

Listen to the cassette. You will hear sentences in Chinese in a different order from the ones below. Write down the number of the Chinese sentence in the box next to its English equivalent.

(a) On Sunday I went shopping in Wanfujing ☐
(b) Last year she went to America ☐
(c) Her mother's friend gave me the ticket yesterday ☐
(d) We have eaten ☐
(e) Here we are! ☐
(f) Have you eaten? ☐

Now listen again and repeat the sentences.

5 Saying you haven't done something

Answer 'no' to all these questions.

MODEL: Nǐ qùle tāde jiā ma?
ANSWER: Méi qù.

(1) Nǐ chī fàn le ma?
(2) Zuótiān qù le Wanfujing ma?
(3) Tā xīngqī èr mǎile dōngxi ma?
(4) Xiǎo Wang hē le jiǔ ma?
(5) Nǐ de péngyǒu lái le ma?
(6) Mǎile Xīan de huǒchē piào ma?

Worth knowing

Hotel accommodation

Since China's decision to become a major tourist destination, hotels have been springing up everywhere. Some, those which are joint ventures with foreign or Hong Kong companies, are of a very high standard, and are priced at the same rates as five-star hotels anywhere else. These hotels are especially good and numerous in Canton, where they were built to cater for the twice-yearly Canton Trade Fair. In other parts of China there are few, if any, luxury hotels; but the standard first-class Chinese hotel is adequate and reasonably comfortable, if shabby. It is a good idea to take a few high-wattage (ie 60W or 100W) light bulbs – buy them in a Chinese shop – with you to hotels outside Beijing, as the reading lights tend to be fitted with 25W bulbs. (This is part of China's attempts to economise on electricity.) Hotels are very good at providing some services, like laundry, but not so good at providing others – such as plumbing that works. As for lower-priced hotels, dormitory beds are now available, and hotels which used to be closed to foreigners are now open to all – if you do not mind spartan simplicity, noise, and complete lack of privacy.

6 Socialising

Key expressions

dānwèi	work unit
wéi!	hullo (on telephone)
Wŏ xiăng hé Feng Cun Li shuō huà	I'd like to talk to Feng Cun Li
Nĭ shì shéi-ah?	Who are you?
Feng Cun Li zài bù zài?	Is Feng Cun Li there? (literally: Feng Cun Li there-not-there?)
Yào bù yào mĭfàn?	Do you want any rice? (literally: Want-not-want rice?)
Yŏu méiyŏu piào?	Are there any tickets? (literally: There-are-there-are-not tickets?)
Kěyĭ qĭng nĭ zhuăngào tā ma?	Can I ask you to give him a message?
Jiàngúo Fàndiànde diànhuà hàomă shì shénme?	What's the phone number of the Jianguo Hotel?
Tā chīfàn qù le	He's gone to eat
Chōu yān ba!	Have a cigarette!
Wŏ bù huì!	I don't (literally: I can't) smoke/drink
Wŏ bù huì shuō Yīngguóhuà	I can't speak English
Nĭ xĭhuān Zhōngguó cài ma?	Do you like Chinese food?

Hěn xǐhuān!	I love it!
Gānbēi!	Cheers!
Wǒ xiǎng dào Xīan qù	I'm thinking of going to Xian

Conversations

1 Jenny is making a telephone call to the *dānwèi* (work unit)[1] where her friend Feng Cun Li works. The man at the other end wants to know what work unit she comes from.

JENNY: Wéi! Wéi![2]
MAN: Wéi!
JENNY: Nǐ hǎo. Wǒ xiǎng hé Feng Cun Li shuō huà.[3]
MAN: Nǐ shì shéi-ah?[4]
JENNY: Wǒ xíng Lo.
MAN: Nǐ shì shénme dānwèi?
JENNY: Wǒ shì Yīngguó huáqiáo – Feng Cun Li zài ma?
MAN: Bù zài.

2 Jenny decides to leave a message for Feng Cun Li.

JENNY: Feng Cun Li bù zài?[5]
MAN: Bù zài. Tā chīfàn[6] qù le.
JENNY: Ah . . . na, kěyǐ qǐng nǐ[7] zhuǎngào tā ma?
MAN: Kěyǐ.
JENNY: Hǎo, wǒ xíng Lo. Wǒ zài Jiàngúo Fàndiàn. Wǒde fángjiān shì 626.
MAN: Jiàngúo Fàndiànde diànhuà hàomǎ shì shénme?
JENNY: 593661.
MAN: 5-9-3-6-6-1 Hǎode, wǒ zhuǎngào tā. Zài jiàn.
JENNY: Xiè xie nǐ. Zài jiàn.

3 Anne Wilson is the guest at a farewell banquet. Lao Wang is her host. They start with tea and cigarettes – though Anne doesn't smoke.

WANG: Anne, nǐ hǎo, nǐ hǎo. Qǐng zùo!
ANNE: Xiè xie nǐ, Lǎo Wang.

WANG: Hē chá ba – wǒmen méiyǒu kāfēi!
ANNE: Zhōngguó chà hěn hǎo – xiè xie nǐ.
WANG: Chōu yān ba![8]
ANNE: Xiè xie – wǒ bù huì.[9]

4 The banquet continues, with Wang performing his duty as host by urging Anne to eat and proposing a toast.

WANG: Anne – chī ba, chī ba.
ANNE: Xiè xie nǐ.
WANG: Nǐ xǐhuān chī Zhōngguó cài ma?[10]
ANNE: Hěn xǐhuān. Yīngguórén dōu xǐhuān chī Zhōngguó cài.
WANG: Shì ma? (The banquet continues until Wang proposes a toast to Anne) Gānbēi!
ANNE: Gānbēi!
GUESTS: Gānbēi! Gānbēi! (Clinking of glasses)

Explanations

1 *Dānwèi*

Most Chinese workers belong to a *dānwèi,* usually translated into English as a 'work unit'. A *dānwèi* can be a school (for the staff: children do not have *dānwèi*), a hospital, ministry, airline or wherever you work. As most people are assigned to their jobs by the government and stay there for life, the *dānwèi* is very important, providing accommodation (sometimes), hospital treatment, holidays and even finding marriage partners. If you are unemployed or self-employed (small traders, bicycle menders, carpenters etc), you do not have a *dānwèi* and life is harder.

2 *Wéi!*

Shout *wéi!* into the telephone when you (finally) get through. The person at the other end will also shout it a few times and then the conversation can begin. *Wéi!* can also be used like the English

'Hey!' to attract attention in crowded shops or restaurants or if you spot a Chinese friend in a crowd.

3 *Wŏ xiăng hé Feng Cun Li shuō huà*

Literally: I'd like with Feng Cun Li talk language.

(a) *Xiăng* means 'think' but is often used to mean 'I'd like to', 'I'm hoping to', 'I'm planning to'.

Wŏ xiăng qù Shànghăi	I'd like to go/I'm planning to go to Shanghai
Feng Cun Li xiăng qù Bĕijīng	Feng Cun Li is thinking of going to Beijing
Wŏ xiăng măi zhè ge huā píng	I'd like to buy this vase

(b) *Shuō huà*

shuō means 'to talk'; *shuō huà* means 'to talk language', i.e. 'to speak'.

Wŏ xiăng hé nĭ shuō huà	I'd like to talk to you
Wŏ huì shuō pŭtōnghuà	I can speak Chinese

4 *Nĭ shì shéi-ah?*

Who are you? (*Shéi* means 'who'.)

The sound *ah* is often heard at the end of sentences. In different parts of China there are regional variations in pronunciation and the length of time the sound lasts. In Cantonese especially it goes on and on! It has no meaning *per se* but simply adds flavour to what is said.

5 *Feng Cun Li zài bù zài?*

'Is Feng Cun Li there?' (Literally, 'Feng Cun Li is there-not-there?')

This way of asking a question is very frequent, and is simplicity itself to form. There is no difference in meaning to a question formed by adding *ma,* but the use of verb + *bù* + verb is perhaps slightly more colloquial.

Nǐ xǐhuan Zhōngguó cài ma?	Do you like Chinese food?
Nǐ xǐhuan bù xǐhuan Zhōngguó cài?	You like-not-like Chinese food?

Gùgōng yuǎn ma?	Is the Forbidden City far?
Gùgōng yuǎn bù yuǎn?	Forbidden City is far-no-far?

We saw in unit 2 that *yǒu* is the only verb in Chinese which forms the negative in the present tense with *méi*. So if you want to use this method of forming a question with *yǒu,* you must use *méi,* not *bù:*

Yǒu píjiǔ ma? *Yǒu méiyǒu píjiǔ?*	Is there any beer?
Nǐ yǒu qián ma? *Nǐ yǒu méiyǒu qiàn?*	Have you any money?

Note: In the past tense, this way of asking questions is not used.

6 *Chīfàn*

Literally, 'to eat rice'; hence 'to eat'. People use the phrase *chīfàn* when they mean 'having a meal'.

The polite enquiry *chīfàn le ma?* ('Have you eaten?') is used almost as a greeting, like 'How are you?' in English. Answer it by saying *Chī le, chī le* ('I've eaten'), unless you actually intend to go off and have a meal with the person who's asked you.

7. *Kěyǐ qǐng nǐ . . .*

Qǐng is used like the English 'please', as in:

qǐng zùo please sit down

qǐng děng yi děng please wait a little

but it actually means 'to request politely'. So *kěyǐ qǐng nǐ . . .* means something like 'is it all right to request you to . . .'

Here is a summary of polite ways to make requests:

Is it allowed? *Xíng ma?* or *Xíng bù xíng?*

Is it OK?	*Kěyǐ ma?* or *Kěyǐ bù kěyǐ?*
Can I ask you?	*Kěyǐ qǐng nǐ . . ?* or *Qǐng wen nǐ. . .?*

8 *Chōu yān ba!*

'Have a cigarette!' *Ba* is used when you are telling or urging someone to do something:

Zǒuba!	Let's go!
Shōuba!	Tell me! (Speak)
Kànba!	Look!

9 *Wǒ bù huì*

(I can't/I'm unable to)

Wǒ bù huì shuō pǔtōnghuà	I can't speak Chinese
Tā bù huì xiě hànze	She can't write Chinese characters
Wǒ bù huì!	I don't! (Used when refusing, for example, a cigarette or some alcohol)

10 *Nǐ xǐhuan Zhōngguó cài ma?*

Do you like Chinese food?

Other examples:

Nǐ xǐhuan Fǎguó cài ma?	Do you like French food?
Tā bù xǐhuan Rìběn cài	She doesn't like Japanese food

The word used for Chinese, French etc. is the same as the name of the country, just as it is for nationalities:

Tāmen shì Déguórén ma?	Are they German?

When referring to the spoken *language* of a country, however, a different word is used, and there are several possibilities:

Wŏ bù huì shuō Yīng	*yŭ* / *wén* / *guóhuà*	I can't speak English
Tá shuō Dé	*yŭ* / *wén* / *guóhuà*	He speaks German

There are no fewer than five names for Mandarin Chinese, and they are all in common use:

pŭtōnghuà – common tongue (the official name for standard Chinese since 1949)

Zhōngguóhuà
Zhōngwén } China language

Hànyŭ – the language of the Han (ethnic Chinese) people

guóyŭ – national language (this name is used outside China, in SE Asia)

Languages (or dialects) of specific regions are called by the place name plus the word *huà* (speech/tongue).

When referring to the *written* language, there is only one possibility:

Tā huì kàn	Fă*wén* / Yīng*wén* / Zhōng*wén*	shū
She can read	French / English / Chinese	books

Notice that when talking about 'western food' in general, i.e. anything non-Chinese, the word used is *cān* (food), not *cài* (dish):

Nĭ xĭhuan bù xĭhuan xī cān?	Do you like western food?

When referring to a specific cuisine, *cai* is used:

Tāmen bù xǐhuan	*Zhōngguó* / *Fǎguó*	*cài*
They don't like	Chinese / French	food

Exercises

1 Phone Conversations

Choose (a) or (b) in each case, to make a typical phone conversation.

(1) YOU: (a) Wéi! Wéi!
(b) Tóngzhìmen hǎo!

(2) LIU: (a) Tā bù zài.
(b) Wéi!

(3) YOU: (a) Nǐ hǎo. Tā zaì ma?
(b) Nǐ hǎo. Wǒ xǐang hé Ma Yuan He shūo huà.

(4) LIU: (a) Aa . . . Ma Yuan He . . . nǐ shì shéi-ah?
(b) Ma Yuan He méi qù Shànghǎi.

(5) YOU: (a) Wǒ xìng Lee. Wǒ shì Yīngguórén.
(b) Jīntiān shì xīngqī sān.

(6) LIU: (a) Duì bù qǐ, Lee xiáojie: Ma Yuan He bù zài.
(b) Lǎo Ma bù huì shuō Yīngwén.

(7) YOU: (a) Nǐ xǐhuān xī cān ma?
(b) Kěyǐ qǐng nǐ zhuǎngào tā ma?

(8) LIU: (a) Kěyǐ, kěyǐ.
(b) Lǎo Ma shì wǒde hǎo péngyǒu.

2 Telephone Numbers

Listen to the cassette and write down the phone numbers of the following places.

(a) British Embassy . . . .

(b) American Embassy . . . .

(c) Beijing Railway Station . . . .

(d) Wanfujing Taxi Company . . . .

(e) Ritan Park Restaurant . . . .

3 When to say what

Match the following phrases with the most appropriate situation. When would you say:

(a) Chīfàn le ma?	(1) When making a phone call
(b) Wǒ xǐang hé Liu Yuan shuō huà	(2) At a meal or banquet
(c) Xiè xie, wǒ bù huì!	(3) When trying to get a ticket
(d) Xīngqī sān, yǒu méiyǒu piào?	(4) When you hope someone will speak English
(e) Gānbēi!	(5) On meeting a friend, just after lunchtime
(f) Nǐ huì shuō Yīngwén ma?	(6) Refusing a cigarette

4 Asking questions

MODEL: *Tā xǐhuan Zhōngguó cài.*

Now form questions in two ways from this sentence:

(i) *Tā xǐhuān zhōngguó cài ma?*
(ii) *Tā xǐhuān bù xǐhuān zhōngguó cài?*

(1) Tāmen mǎi huǒchē piào.

(2) Nǐmen qù Wanfujing mǎi dōngxi.

(3) Lǎo Wang xǐhuān xīcān.

(4) Yǒu jīntiānde piào.

(5) Tā yào hē kāfēi.

(6) Xǐao Liu shì běifāngrén.

(7) Nǐ xiǎng qù Shànghǎi.

5 Asking how many

Remember to use *jǐ* + measure word for nouns, except for *duō shǎo qián?* (money) and *duō shǎo shíjiān?* (time). Now write the questions to which the following are answers:

MODEL: Answer: *Liăng píng*
You write: Yào *jĭ píng* (píjiŭ)?

(1) Măi sì zhāng (piào).
(2) Yào liăng ge xīngqī.
(3) Yī yè yī băi wŭ shí kuài qián.
(4) Yào yī shuāng (kuàizi).
(5) Wŏ érzi liu suile.
(6) Yào liăng (wăn).
(7) Yŏu sān ge (rén).
(8) Măi yī fèn (bào).
(9) Yào sì bĕn (shū).
(10) Yào wŭ ge fángjiān.

6 Say it in Chinese

(1) Yesterday I went to Wanfujing, today I think I'll go to Tienanmen.
(2) Lao Xu doesn't like Western food, he only eats Chinese food.
(3) Who are you? What's your surname?
(4) What's the telephone number of the Xian Guesthouse?
(5) I can't speak German.
(6) Please could I leave a message for Tian Yong?
(7) Ma Yuan He is my old friend.
(8) Xiao Li's work unit is a very good one.
(9) My father and mother like Beijing very much.
(10) Do you take rénmínbì? I haven't any FECs left!

Now compare your answers with the cassette.

Using the phone in China

There are few telephones in China – around six million lines in 1986 – so most people don't have private phones and if you want to talk to them it is easier to phone them at their work unit (*dānwèi*). As the system is so overcrowded it can be difficult (sometimes impossible) to get a free line, and the quality of the line can be very bad. An added complication is that the person who answers the phone is highly unlikely to be the person you want to talk to, as there is generally only one phone for a whole work unit. Finding a phone in the street is not easy, and there are few public phone booths as we know them. But public phones do exist, usually on a table in the street with a small sign above them, and they are closely watched over by a full-time telephone guardian. Otherwise, the main post offices and all big hotels have telephones. Phoning abroad is easy and the line is remarkably clear; most international operators speak English. China has put the modernisation of its telephone exchanges high on the list of priorities, and within a few years will move from having one of the world's oldest and worst systems to one of the world's most modern and best equipped. Till then – keep dialling!

Banquets

Banquets are an essential part of life in China, for the tourist, business person, or other visitor – only the backpacker will escape them. Banquets are not as formal or as costly as they once were, but are still frequent. The banquet begins with the host (rarely hostess – women are still under-represented in higher positions in China) offering the guest(s) of honour tea and cigarettes, while polite small talk is made. Then they proceed to the table, where the host will signal the start of the meal by putting a few tasty morsels of food on the guest's plate. You don't have to eat everything that is put on your plate: if you have had enough, or if you don't like the look of some creature of the deep which you consider would have done better to have stayed where it belonged, just don't eat it; no need to say anything. The meal starts with cold dishes, and continues with at least as many hot dishes as there are guests. It may finish with soup and fruit, and if there is any fruit left over your host may insist on you taking it home with you. As for the toasts – normally the host makes a speech and proposes a toast signalled by the immortal words *gānbēi* (literally, 'empty glasses'). The guest makes a speech in return, either a little later on or at the end of the meal. When all the dishes have been eaten, the host shakes hands all round and everyone vanishes with astounding (and, to a Westerner, rather disconcerting) speed. If you are working in China, you will at some point be expected to host a return banquet.

Making friends

The days when it was dangerous even to speak to a foreigner, and when visiting the home of a Chinese acquaintance was out of the question unless accompanied by the local party secretary, are well and truly gone. The Chinese are extremely friendly and eager to talk – in Chinese, or in English, which many people are learning. The old image of inscrutability is utterly false – only perhaps in lengthy business negotiations do they play their cards close to their chest, and in everyday life their warmth, sincerity and relaxed informality will surprise and delight the visitor. Almost anything may be freely discussed these days – the only taboos are things which are considered private, like sex and marital relations. Politics is no longer taboo, although people may be hesitant to discuss politics if strangers are present. They will not be hesitant about discussing money (much more openly than in the West) and will also prove to be much better informed about foreign affairs than many a Westerner. China now has extensive news coverage of the world beyond the Middle Kingdom, including a nightly, one-hour TV news bulletin in English and a daily paper in English, the *China Daily*.

Appendix

Numbers

Numerals in Chinese are written in both the traditional way, using Chinese characters, and in the Western way: all Chinese are familiar with both.

Here are the numbers 1 – 1 million. They are on the cassette, to help you learn the pronunciation, and there are some exercises afterwards to help you remember them.

Cardinal numbers

0 *líng*
1 *yī*
2 *èr*
3 *sān*
4 *sì*
5 *wŭ*
6 *liù*
7 *qī*
8 *bā*
9 *jiŭ*
10 *shí*
11 *shí yī*
12 *shí èr*
13 *shí sān*
14 *shí sì*
15 *shí wŭ*
16 *shí liù*
17 *shí qī*
18 *shí bā*
19 *shí jiŭ*
20 *èr shí*
21 *èr shí yī*
22 *èr shí èr*
23 *èr shí sān*
24 *èr shí sì*
25 *èr shí wŭ*
26 *èr shí liù*
27 *èr shí qī*
28 *èr shí bā*
29 *èr shí jiŭ*
30 *sān shí*
31 *sān shí yī*
32 *sān shí èr*
33 *sān shí sān*
40 *sì shí*
41 *sì shí yī*
42 *sì shí èr*
50 *wŭ shí*
51 *wŭ shí yī*
52 *wŭ shí èr*
60 *liù shí*
61 *liù shí yī*
70 *qī shí*
80 *bā shí*
90 *jiŭ shí*
100 *yī băi*
101 *yī băi líng yī*
102 *yī băi líng èr*
110 *yī băi yī shí*
120 *yī băi èr shí*

130	*yī bǎi sān shí*	1000	*yī qiān*
140	*yī bǎi sì shí*	2000	*èr qiān*
150	*yī bǎi wǔ shí*	2100	*èr qiān yī bǎi*
160	*yī bǎi liù shí*	2555	*èr qiān wǔ bǎi wǔ shí wǔ*
170	*yī bǎi qī shí*	3000	*sān qiān*
180	*yī bǎi bā shí*	4000	*sì qiān*
190	*yī bǎi jiǔ shí*	5000	*wǔ qiān*
200	*èr bǎi*	10 000	*yī wàn*
300	*sān bǎi*	20 000	*liǎng wàn*
400	*sì bǎi*	30 000	*sān wàn*
500	*wǔ bǎi*	100 000	*shí wàn*
600	*liù bǎi*	200 000	*èr shí wàn*
700	*qī bǎi*	500 000	*wǔ shí wàn*
800	*bā bǎi*	1 000 000	*bǎi wàn*
900	*jiǔ bǎi*		

Ordinal numbers

1st	*dì yī*
2nd	*dì èr*
3rd	*dì sān*
4th	*dì sì*
5th	*dì wǔ*
once	*yí cì*
twice	*liǎng cì*
three times	*sān cì*

Note: Ten thousand in Chinese is used as a unit: for example, your guide will tell you that about *70 000 [qī wàn] ge rèn* built the Great Wall. Sometimes the translation of *(yī) wàn* gets confused and you may be told, for example, that 70 million people built the Great Wall! It is worth remembering this possible confusion when large numbers are being bandied about.

Exercises

1 Recognising the numbers 1 – 100

Listen to the cassette. Write down the numbers in

the order you hear them.

(a) ☐	(d) ☐	(g) ☐	(j) ☐	(m) ☐
(b) ☐	(e) ☐	(h) ☐	(k) ☐	(n) ☐
(c) ☐	(f) ☐	(i) ☐	(l) ☐	(o) ☐

2 **Telephone numbers**

Here is a list of hotels. Next to each one write down the phone number as you hear it on the cassette. Remember that zero is *líng*. In Beijing, when giving phone numbers, the number *one* is usually pronounced *'yāo'* not *'yī'*.

(1) Peking Hotel ....

(2) Xian Guesthouse ....

(3) White Swan Hotel ....

(4) China Hotel ....

(5) Shanghai Mansions ....

(6) Peace Hotel ....

(7) Suzhou Hotel ....

(8) Hangzhou Hotel ....

3 **Dates**

How would you say these dates in Chinese?

(a) 2nd September 1951
(b) 9th January 1829
(c) 24th December 1989
(d) 4th May 1943
(e) 31st November 1898
(f) 1st January 1997

4 **Money** (see unit 2)

Listen to the price of each item and label it. The items are in a different order on the cassette – just to add a bit of spice!

How much is . . .

(1) . . . that big teapot?

(2) . . . the plane ticket to Guangzhou?

(3) . . . a hotel room, per night?

(4) . . . this book by Lu Xun?

(5) . . . the newspaper?
(6) . . . a bus ticket to Tienanmen?
(7) . . . that hat?
(8) . . . this vase?

5 **Times** (see unit 4)

Listen to the cassette. What times do these events take place?

(a) The Shanghai train leaves at . . . .
(b) I will phone you at . . . .
(c) The plane for Beijing leaves at . . . .
(d) The bus to Badheide arrives at . . . .
(e) Xiao Liu is coming at . . . .

6 **Large numbers**

How would you express these large numbers in Chinese? (N.B. All these statistics are approximate)

(a) The population of Shanghai (12 million people).
(b) The number of bicycles in Beijing (4 million).
(c) The number of students in Beijing (94 000).
(d) The number of rooms in the Forbidden City (9999).
(e) The altitude of Lhasa (3600 metres).
(f) The length of the Yangtse River (5525 km).

Weights and measures

The metric system has been used throughout China since 1949. (Before that time, weights and measures were slightly different in each town.)

yī lí mǐ	one centimetre
yì mǐ/yī gōng chǐ	one metre
yī gōnglǐ	one kilometre
yī gōngjīn	one kilogram
yī jīn	500 grams
bàn jīn	250 grams

(The word *gōng* means 'public' and is used to show the metric system is now the standard system.)

Colours

black	*hēi sè*	purple	*zǐ sè*
blue	*lán sè*	red	*hóng sè*
brown	*hè sè*	silver	*yín sè*
golden	*jīn sè*	turquoise	*qīng lù sè*
green	*lù sè*	white	*bái sè*
orange	*jú hóng sè*	yellow	*huáng sè*
grey	*huī sè*		

Age

It is quite normal for Chinese people who chat to you on trains or in parks to ask your age, be you male or female, 25 or 65. They find it quite hard to guess the age of foreign faces so you can always lie! If you are to guess their age it is polite to knock a few years off what you really think . . . which since many Chinese look 10 years younger than they are will come quite naturally!

Nǐ jǐ suì?	How old are you? (Note: *nián*, the word for a calendar year, is not used in talking about age)
Wǒ érshí yī suì	I'm 21 (years old)
(Wǒde) érzi wǔ suì	(My) son's five (years old)

Seasons

Spring	*Chūntiān*
Summer	*Xiàtiān*
Autumn	*Qiūtiān*
Winter	*Dōngtiān*
In spring	*Zài chūntiān*
In summer	*Zài xiàjì*
In autumn	*Zài qiūtiān*
In winter	*Zài dōngjì*

Quick reference sections

Don't forget to arm yourself with a good pocket dictionary/phrasebook as *Get By in Chinese* cannot hope to cover all the vocabulary you will need. Here are a few expressions which have not occurred in the six units but which you may need.

Clarification and help

What is this called?	*Zhè jiào shénme?*
What does this mean?	*Zhè shì shénme yì si?*
I don't understand	*Wǒ bù dǒng*
I don't know	*Wǒ bù zhīdào*
Please speak slowly	*Qǐng nǐ màn màn de shuō*
Can you help me?	*Kěyǐ bāng zhù wǒ mā?*

Needs

Where's the lavatory?	*Cèsuǒ zài nǎr?*
I need a doctor	*Wǒ jí xū yí wèi dài fū*
I'm not feeling well	*Wǒ júe de bù shū fu*
Help!	*Jiù rén!*
Fire!	*Huǒ!*
It's broken	*Zhè ge huài le* (used of appliances etc. – not limbs)
Leave me alone!	*Bié guǎn wǒ!*

Floors

Chinese buildings are the same system as the USA: i.e. the British 'ground floor' is their 'first floor'.

(On the) first floor	*(zài) yī lóu*
(On the) second floor	*(zài) èr lóu*
Upstairs	*lóu shàng*
Downstairs	*lóu xìa*

Further study

The Centre for Information on Language Teaching (C.I.L.T.) publish a complete list of courses and course books available in Britain for the study of Chinese. Contact them at Regent's College, Inner Circle, Regent's Park, London NW1.
Tel: 01-486 8221.

Key to exercises

Unit 1

1 (a) Nǐmen hǎo!
(b) Nǐ hǎo, Xiǎo Liu.
(c) Nǐ hǎo, Lǎo Zhang.
(d) Nǐ hǎo, Deng Lǎo.

2 (a) Tā xìng Thomas. Tā shì Yīngguórén.
(b) Tā xìng Dupont. Tā shì Fǎguórén.
(c) Tā xìng Wang. Tā shì Měiguó huáqiáo.
(d) Tā xìng Li. Tā shì Zhōngguórén.

3 (a) Nǐ shì Měiguórén ma?
(b) Nǐ shì huáqiáo ma?
(c) Nǐ shì Shànghǎirén ma?

4 (a) Shì/Bù shì.
(b) Shì/Bù shì.
(c) Wǒ xìng (surname).

5 (a) Nǐ hǎo Xiǎo Liu
Nǐmen hǎo, Lǎo Wang, Xiǎo Feng.
(b) Nǐ hǎo. Wǒ xìng Wang.
Nǐ hǎo. Wǒ xìng Wilson.
(c) Nǐ shì Měiguórén ma?
Bù. Wǒ shì Yīngguórén.

6 (a) Tà shì Yīngguórén ma?
(b) Lǎo Wang shì Běijìngrén ma?
(c) Tāmen shì Zhōngguórén ma?
(d) Nǐ xìng Liu ma?
(e) Tāmen bù shì Měiguórén ma?

7 (a) Anne shì Měiguórén ma? Bù shì – (*or*: bù) tā shì Yīngguórén.
(b) Lǎo Wang shì Shànghǎirén ma? Bù shì – (*or*: bù) tā shì Tiānjīnrén.
(c) Tāmen shì Běijīngrén ma? Bù – tāmen shì Nánjīngrén.
(d) Nǐ shì Fǎguórén ma? Bù – wǒ shì Déguórén.

Unit 2

1 (a) Fish . . . Yes
(b) Qingdao beer . . . Yes
(c) Vegetables . . . Yes
(d) Rice . . . Yes
(e) Noodles . . . No
(f) Coca-Cola . . . No
(g) Dumplings . . . No
(h) Shanghai beer . . . Yes

2 (a) 4
(b) 7
(c) 2
(d) 6
(e) 8
(f) 3
(g) 1
(h) 5

3 Xiáojie duì bù qǐ; hái yào . . .
(a) . . . yī píng Qingdao píjiǔ.
(b) . . . yī bēi kāfēi.
(c) . . . yī shuāng kuàizi.
(d) . . . yī bēi chá.
(e) . . . liǎng wǎn miàntiáo.
(f) . . . sān bēi kāfēi.

4 (a) Tā shì Zhōngguórén ma?
Tā bù shì Zhōngguórén.
(b) Tā yào sì bēi chà ma?
Tā bù yào sì bēi chà.
(c) Yǒu píjiǔ ma?
Méiyǒu píjiǔ.
(d) Tāmen shì Shànghǎirén ma?
Tāmen bù shì Shànghǎirén.
(e) Nǐmen yào sān bēi kāfēi ma?
Nǐmen bù yaò sān bēi kāfēi.
(f) Wǒmen yào sān píng Shànghǎi pìjiǔ ma?
Wǒmen bù yào sān píng Shànghǎi píjiǔ.
(g) Yǒu mǐfàn ma?
Méiyǒu mǐfàn.

5 5 – c
4 – e
2 – b
3 – f
6 – d
1 – a

6 (1) Qǐng gěi wǒ liǎng píng píjiǔ; hái yào liǎng bēi kāfēi.
(2) Tā bù shì Zhōngguórén, tā shì Měiguó huáqiáo.
(3) Mǐfàn méiyǒule; miàntiáo yě méiyǒule.
(4) Wǒ bù yào jiǔ. Qǐng gěi wǒ yī bēi chá.
(5) Xiǎo péngyǒu, nǐ yào yī píng Kělè ma?
(6) Hái yǒu yú ma?
(7) Qǐng děng yī xiàr/děng yi děng.
(8) Qǐng zuò.

Unit 3

1 (a) Where's the Forbidden City?
(b) Is Xiao Liu there?
(c) Where's your home?
(d) Is Jenny in Beijing?
(e) They aren't in Shanghai.
(f) Where can I buy a vase?

2 2 – d
3 – e
1 – c
4 – b
5 – a

3 (a) 4
(b) 1
(c) 5
(d) 2
(e) 6
(f) 8
(g) 3
(h) 7

4 (i) Běijīng Fàndiàn
(ii) Běijīng Fàndiàn
(iii) běi
(iv) Bù yuǎn
(v) Běijīng Fàndiàn
(vi) gōng gòng
(vii) sì (4)
(viii) Gōng gòng

5 (1) Qù *Nánjīng dōng lù* zǒu nǎ lù gōng gòng qì chē?
Nos. 2-5. Substitute place names as appropriate.

6 A. (1) Chá hú duō shǎo qiān?
(2) Shí kuài wǔ máo sān fēn qián.
Shí kuài wǔ máo sān.
B. (1) Yī wǎn mǐfàn duō shǎo qiān?
(2) Sān máo qián.
Sān máo.
C. (1) Huā píng duō shǎo qián?
(2) Jiǔ kuài líng wǔ fēn qián.
Jiǔ kuài líng wǔ.
D. (1) Chá bēi duō shǎo qián?
(2) Qī kuài liǎng máo qián.
Qī kuài liǎng máo. (Note: after *liǎng* the unit is always used)

7 1 – a
2 – b
3 – a
4 – a
5 – a
6 – a
7 – a

8 (1) (a) Dōngfāng Fàndiàn zài nàr? (b) Yuǎn ma?
(2) (a) Nǐ jiā zài Běijīng ma? (b) Yuǎn ma? (c) Nǐ shì Běifāngrén ma?
(3) (a) Kěyǐ kàn kan zhè ge huā píng ma? (b) Duō shǎo qián?
(4) (a) Qù Gùgōng zùo nǎ lù gōng gòng qì chē? (b) Gōng gòng qì chē zhàn zài nǎr?
(5) (a) Gùgōng yuǎn ma? (b) Yī zhāng piào duō shǎo qián?

Unit 4

1 A 0845
B 1405
C 1830
D 1655
E 0615

2 A. Qù Fuzhōude fēijī jǐ diǎn qǐ fěi?
Shàngwǔ qī diǎn wǔ shí wǔ fēn.
Jǐ diǎn dào Fuzhōu?
Shàngwǔ shí diǎn sì shí wǔ fēn.

B. Qù Guǎngzhōude fēijī jǐ diǎn qǐ fěi?
Shàngwǔ jiǔ diǎn sān shí fēn/jiǔ diǎn bàn.
Jǐ diǎn dào Guǎngzhōu?
Xiàwǔ shí èr diǎn èr shí fēn.

C. Qù Guilinde fēijī jǐ diǎn qǐ fěi?
Xiàwǔ yī diǎn wǔ shí wǔ fēn.
Jǐ diǎn dào Guilin?
Sì diǎn sì shí wǔ fēn.

D. Qù Xiāng Gǎngde fēijī jǐ diǎn qǐ fěi?
Xiàwǔ sì diǎn yī kè/shí wǔ fēn.
Jǐ diǎn dào Xiāng Gǎng?
Wǎnshàng liù diǎn èr shí wǔ fēn.

E. Qù Lundunde fēijī jǐ diǎn qǐ fěi?
Xiàwǔ wǔ diǎn sì shí wǔ fēn.
Jǐ diǎn dào Lundun?
Liù diǎn wǔ shí wǔ fēn.

F. Qù Bàlide fēijī jǐ diǎn qǐ fěi?
Wǎnshàng qī diǎn sì shí wǔ fēn.
Jǐ diǎn dào Bàli?
Zǎoshàng liù diǎn wǔ shí wǔ fēn.

3 (1) h
(2) e
(3) a
(4) i
(5) c
(6) d
(7) f
(8) b
(9) g
(10) j

4 (b) Yī jiǔ sān jiǔ nián jiǔ yuè sān hào.
(c) Shí èr yuè èr shí wǔ hào.
(e) Yī jiǔ yī bā nián.

5 Your itinerary should read something like this:

Beijing	plane	4.00 pm Sunday	Forbidden City	Jiangguo Hotel
Xian	train	3.30 pm Wednesday	Terracotta Army	Xian Guesthouse
Turfan	train	9.00 pm Sunday	Dunhuang Grottoes	Turfan Guesthouse
Urumqi	train	8.15 am Tuesday	West Market	Yanan Hotel
Kunming	plane	2.30 pm Friday	Dianchi Lake	Kunming Hotel
Hong Kong	plane	4.30 pm Monday	Shopping	Marco Polo Hotel

6 (a) Nǐ hǎo. Wǒ yào qù Xīan.
(b) Xīngqī sān yǒu piào ma?
(c) Xīngqī wǔ yǒu piào ma/kěyǐ ma?
(d) Hǎode! Qǐng gěi wǒ sì zhāng.
(e) Ruǎnxí.
(f) Rénmínbì xíng ma?
(g) Gěi nǐ 420 kuài (qián). Huǒchē jǐ diǎn kāi?
(h) Jǐ diǎn dào Xīan?

Unit 5

1 (1) My younger sister's husband bought the train tickets yesterday.
(2) Lao Zhang's wife is a southerner.
(3) Is this today's paper?
(4) Whose is this glass of beer?
(5) Is this your book?
(6) In my house there are only two rooms – one big one, one small one.
(7) The big one's yours, the small one's Lao Wang's.
(8) I bought two teapots – an expensive one and a cheap one.

2 3 – c
2 – d
4 – b
1 – a

3 (1) Jīntiān tài rèle!
(2) Běijīng tài lěngle!
(3) (Wǒ) tài lèile!
(4) Tā tài hǎole!
(5) Tāde zhàngfū tài lǎole!
(6) Zhè ge fángjiān tài guìle!
(7) Zhè ge huāpíng tài dàle!
(8) Zhè ge chá hú tài xiǎole!

4 (a) 6 (b) 1
(c) 3 (d) 4
(e) 5 (f) 2

5 (1) Méi chī/Méiyǒu
(2) Méi qù/Méiyǒu
(3) Méi mǎi/Méiyǒu
(4) Méi hē/Méiyǒu
(5) Méi lái/Méiyǒu
(6) Méi mǎi/Méiyǒu

Unit 6

1 (1) a
(2) b
(3) b
(4) a
(5) a
(6) a
(7) b
(8) a

2 (a) 5321961 (b) 5323830
(c) 554866 (d) 550221
(e) 592648

3 (a) 5 (b) 1
(c) 6 (d) 3
(e) 2 (f) 4

4 (1) Tāmen mǎi huǒchē piào ma?
Tāmen mǎi bù mǎi huǒchē piào?

(2) Nǐmen qù Wanfujing mǎi dōngxi ma?
Nǐmen qù bù qù Wanfujing mǎi dōngxi?

(3) Lǎo Wang xǐhuān xīcān ma?
Lǎo Wang xǐhuān bù xǐhuān xīcān?

(4) Yǒu jīntiānde piào ma?
Yǒu méiyǒu jīntiānde piào?

(5) Tā yào hē kāfēi ma?
Tā yào bù yào hē kāfēi?

(6) Xiăo Liu shì bĕifāngrén ma?
Xiăo Liu shì bù shì bĕifāngrén?

(7) Nĭ xiăng qù Shànghăi ma?
Nĭ xiăng bù xiăng qù Shànghăi?

5 (1) Măi jĭ zhāng?
(2) Yào duō shăo shíjīan?
(3) Yī yè duō shăo qián?
(4) Yào jĭ shuāng?
(5) Nĭ érzi jĭ sui le?
(6) Yào jĭ wăn?
(7) Yŏu jĭge rén?
(8) Măi jĭ fèn?
(9) Yào jĭ bĕn?
(10) Yào jĭge fáng jiān.

6 (1) Zuótiān wŏ dào Wánfŭjĭng qùle (wŏ qùle Wánfŭjĭng): jīntiān wŏ xiăng dào Tiānānmén qù (wŏ xiăng qù Tiānānmén).
(2) Lăo Xu bù xĭhuān xīcān; tā zhĭ xĭhuān Zhōngguó cài.
(3) Nĭ shì shéi-ah? Nĭ xìng shénme?
(4) Xīan Bīnguănde diànhuà hàomă shì shénme?
(5) Wŏ bù huì shuō Déyŭ/Déguóhuà.
(6) Kĕyĭ qĭng nĭ zhuăngào Tian Yong ma?
(7) Ma Yuan He shì wŏde lăo péngyou.
(8) Xiăo Lide dānwèi hĕn hăo.
(9) Wŏ māma, bāba, hĕn xĭhuān Bĕijīng.
(10) Rénmínbì xíng ma? Wàihùi méiyŏule!

Key to exercises in the appendix

1 Numbers 1 – 100

(a) 23
(b) 14
(c) 91
(d) 82
(e) 64
(f) 71
(g) 40
(h) 68
(i) 7
(j) 17
(k) 39
(l) 22
(m) 12
(n) 15
(o) 50

2 Phone numbers

1. 558331
2. 51351
3. 886968
4. 666888
5. 246260
6. 211244
7. 4646
8. 22921

3 Dates

(a) yī jiǔ wǔ yī nián jiǔ yuè èr hào
(b) yī bā èr jiǔ nián yī yuè jiǔ hào
(c) yī jiǔ bā jiǔ nián shí èr yuè èrshí sì hào
(d) yī jiǔ sì sān nián wǔ yuè sì hào
(e) yī bā jiǔ bā nián shí yī yuè sānshí yī hào
(f) yī jiǔ jiǔ qī nián yī yuè yī hào

4

1. Bus ticket	¥0.33
2. Hotel room	¥69
3. Vase	¥15.50
4. Newspaper	¥0.5
5. Hat	¥9.60
6. Plane ticket	¥325
7. Book	¥2.30
8. Teapot	¥8.25

5 Times

(a) 19.15
(b) 10.00
(c) 16.45
(d) 18.10
(e) 20.30

6 (a) yī qiān èr bǎi wàn ge rén
(b) sì bǎi wàn ge zì xíng chē
(c) jiǔ wàn sì qiān ge xuésheng
(d) jiǔ qiān jiǔ bǎi jiǔshi jiǔ ge fángjiān
(e) sān qiān liù bǎi mǐ/gōngchǐ
(f) wǔ qiān wǔ bǎi èr shí wǔ gōnglǐ

Word list

Vocabulary

Words which appear in the appendix are not listed here.

Chinese/English

A	*Aìerlán*	Ireland
	aìrén	loved one (spouse)
	āyí	auntie
B	*ba*	(particle of suggestion or advice)
	bàba	father
	bào	newspaper
	bēi	cup
	běi	north
	běifāngrén	northerner
	běn	volume (measure word for book)
	bǐ	pen
	bīnguǎn	hotel (guesthouse)
	bù	no, not
C	*cài*	vegetables, dish
	caìdān	menu
	cān	food
	chá	tea
	chá bēi	teacup
	chá hú	teapot
	cháng	long
	chīfàn	eat
	chōu yān ba!	have a cigarette!
D	*dà*	big
	dàjīe	avenue
	dānwèi	work unit
	dào	to, reach, arrive
	dǎ suàn	plan
	Déguó	Germany
	děng	wait
	diànhuà	telephone
	dìdi	brother (younger)
	dōng	east
	dōngxi	things
	dōu	all
	duì bù qǐ	sorry
E	*érzi*	son
F	*Fǎguó*	France
	fàndiàn	hotel

	fēijī	aeroplane
	fēijī chǎng	airport
	fèn	copy (measure word for newspaper)
	fēnzhōng	minute
	fú wù yuán	service personnel
	fūren	wife
G	*gānbēi!*	cheers!
	gēge	brother (older)
	gěi	give
	gōng	palace
	gōng gòng qì chē	bus
	gōng yuán	park
	gūanxi	connection
	guì	expensive
H	*hái*	still, yet, any more
	hǎi	sea
	háishi	or, either
	Hànyu	Chinese language
	hànze	Chinese characters
	hǎo	good
	hào	number (bus, dates)
	hàomǎ	number (telephone, room number)
	hé	and, with
	hěn	very
	hǔ	lake
	huānyíng	welcome
	huā píng	vase
	huáqiáo	overseas Chinese
	huì	can (be able to)
	huǒchē	train
	huǒchē zhàn	railway station
J	*jǐ*	how many
	jiā	family
	jiǎozi	dumplings
	jǐ diǎn	what time
	jiějie	sister (older)
	jīntiān	today
	jiù	then
	jiǔ	alcohol
K	*kāfēi*	coffee
	kāi	start
	kāishuǐ	boiled water
	kàn	see, read
	kànkan	have a look
	kěyǐ	OK, fine
	kuàizi	chopsticks
L	*lái*	come
	lǎo	old

	lèi	tired
	lěng	cold
	liǎng	two
	líng	tomb
	lù	street
M	*ma*	(question particle)
	mǎi	buy
	māma	mother
	Měiguó	USA
	méi guānxi	never mind
	mèimei	younger sister
	méiyǒu	there's none
	miàntiáo	noodles
	mǐfàn	rice
	míngtiān	tomorrow
N	*nà*	that, those
	nǎ lù	which (bus)
	nán	south
	ne	how about
	nián	year
	nǐde	your, yours
	nǐmen	you (plural)
	nǐmende	yours (plural)
	nǚér	daughter
P	*péngyǒu*	friend
	piào	ticket
	píenyì	cheap
	píjiǔ	beer
	pútaojiǔ	wine
	pǔtōnghuà	Chinese (Mandarin)
Q	*qián*	money
	qǐ fēi	take off (planes)
	qǐng	please, to request
	qīngcài	(green) vegetables
R	*rè*	hot
	rénmínbì	Chinese currency
	ruǎnxí/ruǎnwò	soft sleeper (trains)
S	*shān*	mountain
	shàngwǔ	a.m.
	shéide	whose
	shénme	what
	shénme shíhou	when
	shì	be (verb)
	shìchǎng	market
	shíjiān	time
	shū	book
	shuāng	pair (measure word)
	shuō	speak
	shūshu	uncle
	Sūgelán	Scotland

T	*tā*	he, she, it
	tāde	his, hers, its
	tài	too
	tāmen	they
	tāmende	their, theirs
	tiān	day
	tiānqì	weather
	tóngzhì/tóngzhìmen	comrade(s)
W	*waìguórén*	foreigner
	waìhuì	Foreign Exchange Certificates
	wàng	towards
	wǎnshàng	evening
	wéi	hullo! (on phones) hey!
	Wēiěrshì	Wales
	wèntí	problem
	wǒ	I
	wǒde	mine, my
	wǒmen	we
	wǒmende	our, ours
X	*xī*	west
	xiǎng	think
	xiānsheng	mister, husband
	xiáojie	miss, mademoiselle
	xiàwǔ	p.m.
	xiě	write
	xiè xie	thank you
	xǐhuān	like
	xìng	be called (surname)
	xíng	be allowed
	xīngqī	week
Y	*yào*	want
	yě	also, too
	yè	night (in hotel)
	yígòng	altogether
	Yīngguó	England
	yìngxí	hard seat (trains)
	yī xiàr	a moment
	yǒu	there is/are
	Yǒuyi Shāngdiàn	Friendship Store
	yú	fish
	yuè	month
Z	*zài*	(be located) in/at
	zài jiàn	goodbye
	zài nǎr	where
	zǎoshàng	early morning
	zhàn	station, (bus) stop
	zhāng	(measure word for ticket)
	zhàngfu	husband
	zhè	this
	zhèr	here

zhī	(measure word for pens, cigarettes)
zhĭ	only
zhōng	central
Zhōngguó	China
zhōngwŭ	noon
zhù	live, stay
zhuăngào	give a message
zì xíng chē	bicycle
zŏuba!	let's go
zuò	sit
zuótiān	yesterday

English/Chinese

A	a.m.	*shàngwŭ* *zaŏshàng*
	aeroplane	*fēijī*
	airport	*fēijī chăng*
	alcohol	*jiŭ*
	all	*dōu*
	allowed	*xíng*
	also	*yĕ*
	altogether	*yígòng*
	America	*Mĕiguó*
	and	*hé*
	arrive	*dào*
	auntie	*āyí*
	avenue	*dàjīe*
B	be	*shì*
	be there	*zài*
	beer	*píjiŭ*
	bicycle	*zì xíng chē*
	big	*dà*
	book	*shū*
	bottle	*píng*
	bowl	*wăn*
	brother	*gēge* (older) *dìdi* (younger)
	bus	*gōng gòng qì chē*
	buy	*măi*
C	(be) called	*xìng (surname)*
	can	*huì*
	central	*zhōng*
	cheap	*piényì*
	cheers!	*gānbēi!*
	China	*Zhōngguó*
	Chinese	*pŭtōnghuà*
	chopsticks	*kuàizi*
	coffee	*kāfēi*

	cold	*lěng*
	come	*lái*
	comrade	*tóngzhì* (*tóngzhìmen* – plural)
	cup	*bēi*
D	daughter	*nǚér*
	day	*tiān*
	drink	*hē*
	drinking water	*kāishuǐ*
	dumplings	*jiǎozi*
E	east	*dōng*
	easy	*róngyì*
	eat	*chīfàn*
	England	*Yīngguó*
	English	*Yīngguóhuà*
	evening	*wǎnshàng*
	expensive	*guì*
F	family	*jiā*
	far	*yuǎn*
	father	*bàba*
	fish	*yú*
	food	*cài* *cān*
	foreigner	*wàiguórén*
	Foreign Exchange Certificates	*wàihuì*
	friend	*péngyǒu*
	Friendship Store	*Yǒuyì Shāngdiàn*
G	Germany	*Déguó*
	give a message	*zhuǎngào*
	go	*qù*
	good	*hǎo*
	goodbye	*zài jiàn*
	guesthouse	*bīnguǎn*
H	hard seats	*yìngzuò*
	hard sleeper	*yìngxí*
	have a look	*kànkan*
	hot	*rè*
	hotel	*fàndiàn*
	how many	*jǐ*
	how much	*duō shǎo*
	hullo	*wéi!* (on telephone) *nǐ(men) hǎo!*
	husband	*xiānsheng, zhàngfu*
I	I	*wǒ*
	in	*zài*
	Ireland	*Aìerlán*
K	know	*zhīdào*
L	lake	*hú*
	like	*xǐhuān*

	live	*zhù*
M	market	*shìchăng*
	miss	*xiáojie*
	mister	*xiānsheng*
	moment	*yī xiàr*
	money	*qián*
	month	*yuè*
	(any) more	*hái*
	mother	*māma*
	mountain	*shān*
	Mrs	*taìtai*
	my, mine	*wŏde*
N	newspaper	*bào*
	night (in hotel)	*yè*
	noodles	*miàntiáo*
	noon	*zhōngwŭ*
	northerner	*bĕifāngrén*
	number (bus)	*hào*
	number (telephone)	*hàomă*
O	OK	*kĕyĭ*
	old	*lăo*
	only	*zhĭ*
	or, either	*háishi*
	overseas Chinese	*huáqiáo*
P	p.m.	*xiàwŭ, wănshàng*
	palace	*gōng*
	park	*gōng yuán*
	pen	*bĭ*
	person/people	*rén*
	plan	*dă suàn*
	please	*qĭng*
	portion	*fèn*
	problem	*wèntí*
R	railway station	*huŏchē zhàn*
	rice	*mĭfàn*
S	Scotland	*Sūgelán*
	see	*kàn*
	(go) shopping	*măi dōngxi*
	sister	*jiĕjie* (older) *mèimei* (younger)
	sit	*zuò*
	small	*xiăo*
	smoke	*chōu yān*
	soft sleeper (trains)	*ruănxí/ruănwò*
	son	*érzi*
	sorry	*duì bù qĭ*
	south	*nán*
	speak	*shuō*
	start	*kāi*
	stay	*zhù*

	street	*lù*
T	take off (planes)	*qǐ fēi*
	tea	*chá*
	teapot	*chá hú*
	telephone	*diànhuà*
	temple	*tán* (Taoist) *miào* (Buddhist)
	thank you	*xiè xie (ni)*
	that	*nà*
	their, theirs	*tāmende*
	then	*jiù*
	there is/are	*yǒu(de)*
	there is/are none	*méiyǒu*
	they	*tāmen*
	things	*dōngxi*
	think	*xiǎng*
	this	*zhè*
	ticket/receipt	*piào*
	time	*shíjiān*
	tired	*lèi*
	to	*dào*
	today	*jīntiān*
	tomb	*líng*
	tomorrow	*míngtiān*
	too	*tài*
	train	*huǒchē*
	travel by	*zuò*
	two (of something)	*liǎng*
U	uncle	*shūshu*
V	vase	*huā píng*
	vegetables	*qīngcài*
	very	*hěn*
W	wait	*děng*
	waiter/waitress	*fú wù yuán*
	Wales	*Wēiěrshì*
	want	*yào*
	water	*shuǐ*
	we	*wǒmen*
	weather	*tiānqì*
	week	*xīngqī*
	welcome	*huānyíng*
	west	*xī*
	what	*shénme*
	what time	*jǐ diǎn*
	when	*shénme shíhou*
	where	*zài nǎr*
	whose	*shéide*
	wife	*taìtai, fūren*
	wine	*pútaojiǔ*
	work unit	*dānwèi*